Active Play!™

Fun Physical Activities for Young Children

Diane H. Craft, PhD
Physical Education Department
State University of New York at Cortland

Craig L. Smith

D1604418

Published by Active Play Books, Cortland, NY 13045 • www.activeplaybooks.com

ISBN-13: 978-0-9826400-0-5

Craft, Diane H. 1950-
Active play! Fun physical activities for young children / Diane H. Craft,
Craig L. Smith

Includes bibliographical references.

Credits:
Cover Design: Doreen Warholic
Interior Design: Craig L. Smith
Photography: Craig L. Smith
DVD Label Design: Doreen Warholic

All music contained on this book's companion DVD, *Active Play! Fun Physical Activities for Young Children*, was written and performed by Paul "Vincent" Nunes. Music copyright Vincent 1991, 1994, 1997, 2001, and 2005. For information about Vincent's CDs, books, keynotes, concerts and workshops visit www.LighthouseRecords.com.

Safety

The information in this book and its supplemental DVD, *Active Play! Fun Physical Activities for Young Children*, was developed with the safety of young children in mind. The book has many suggestions for the safe enjoyment of the activities it describes. It needs to be read in its entirety by the adult supervising the young children before they enjoy these activities.

In all activities, caregivers must observe the children at all times. Be especially watchful that children do not modify pieces of equipment to create choking or other physical hazards. Do not use equipment that poses a risk to young children, or in a way that is not intended. Supervise children closely when engaged in activities that use balloons, small objects, or water to prevent suffocation or drowning. Provide safe play areas because young children engaged in physical activities become very focused on their tasks and are not especially aware of their surroundings.

While we have given thorough consideration to safety, we cannot anticipate how the information we present will be used, and therefore we disclaim liability for its improper or negligent use.

Acknowledgments

Thank you to Cortland County and the Bronx, New York, family childcare providers for allowing us to work with you in the development of the activities in this book. We appreciate your gracious hospitality and flexibility as we videoed, photographed and played these physical activities with the children in your homes. It was our great fortune to work with all of you.

Thank you to the children, and their families, with whom we led these activities. It was such fun learning from you!

Thank you to Renée McCall, an exceptionally talented adapted physical educator, who has taught Diane so much about helping preschoolers experience joy and purpose through physical activities.

Diane H. Craft and Craig L. Smith

Contents

GAME FINDER

These Physical Activities Work On:

Listing of Physical Activities	Page number	Object, color, shape recognition	Spatial relationships	Locomotor skills	Object control skills	Stability	Cardiovascular endurance	Muscular strength and endurance
All Stop & Go to Music	34			X			X	
Alligator Pit	35					X		
Bubble Wrap Jumping	36			X			X	
Clean Out the Back Yard: Kicking	37				X		X	
Clean Out the Back Yard: Throwing	38				X		X	
Clean Up the Floor	40				X		X	
Color Challenge	41	X					X	
Easy Catching	42				X			
Easy Kicking	43				X			
Easy Punching	44				X			
Easy Striking	45				X			
Egg Farmer	46			X		X		
Feed the Penguin	47			X		X		
Float the Fish	48				X	X		
Frog Catcher	50			X		X	X	X
Garden Friends	51		X	X				
Go Fishing	52	X		X				
Healthy Food Hunting	53	X		X				

These Physical Activities Work On:

Listing of Physical Activities	Page number	Object, color, shape recognition	Spatial relationships	Locomotor skills	Object control skills	Stability	Cardiovascular endurance	Muscular strength and endurance
Hoop Bus	55			X				
Hoop Chase	56			X	X			
Hoop Limbo	57					X		
Hoop Right Through	58	X	X			X		
Hoop Scatterball	59			X				
Hoop Scotch	60			X	X	X		
Hoop Target	61				X			
Jump & Shop	62	X		X		X		
Land/Lake	63			X			X	
Laundry Pick-Up	64			X				
Letter to a Friend	65			X				
Lug-a-Jug	66					X		X
Matching Numbers	67	X		X				
Matching Socks	69	X		X				
Musical Hoops	70			X				
Newspaper Toss	71				X			
Obstacle Course: Indoor	72		X	X		X		X
Obstacle Course: Outdoor	75		X	X		X		X

These Physical Activities Work On:

Listing of Physical Activities	Page number	Object, color, shape recognition	Spatial relationships	Locomotor skills	Object control skills	Stability	Cardiovascular endurance	Muscular strength and endurance
Obstacle Course: Over, Under, Through	78		X			X		
On/Off	80		X	X				
Paper Plate Scooters	81					X		X
Push & Pull Baskets	82							X
Puzzle Carry	83	X		X				
Rainbow Pieces	84	X				X		
Running with Streamers	85			X			X	
Sock Plows	86					X		X
Sock Tails	87					X	X	
Sock the Cans	88				X			
Sock'n Smiley	90				X			
Spiders & Bugs	91					X	X	X
Stilt Blocks	92					X		
Stocking Grocery Shelves	93					X		X
Swat the Fly	94				X		X	
Zoom, Zoom, Zoom	96						X	

Importance of
Physical Activity

Today's preschoolers might not live as long as their parents do because of the effects of obesity.

There is an epidemic of childhood obesity in our nation. The percentage of preschool children who are overweight has more than doubled between 1971 and 2004 (Ogden et al., 2007)

Year	Overweight Preschoolers
1971	5.8%
2002	10.3%
2004	13.9%

Research shows that many overweight preschoolers are likely to become even fatter because they are not playing hard during the preschool day (Trost et al., 2003). For the first time in the history of this country, today's preschoolers might not live as long as their parents do because of the effects of obesity. This is because many of today's young children have unhealthy eating habits and don't get enough active play.

It wasn't always this way. Children used to come home from school and eat a small snack. Then they would go outside and play hard until called in for dinner. They ate healthy foods. Very few children were overweight. Today, many children come home from school and sit quietly in front of TVs and computer screens. They eat unhealthy snack foods and drink soda, waiting for parents to come home from work. They watch countless TV ads telling them 'it's fun going to fast food restaurants.' Eating unhealthy foods made 'just for children' has become common. They eat many more sweets and fats and are far less active than the children of forty years ago. As a result, today's children are getting heavier and heavier – and at younger and younger ages.

Q: What health problems might young children face if they eat too many calories and are not physically active?

A: Overweight children are more likely to have type 2 diabetes, high blood pressure, bone and joint problems, and weak immune systems. They are more likely to sleep poorly and to be teased by other children about their weight. Young children can already have risk factors for heart disease. Physical activity can reduce these risk factors.

Most children who are overweight in preschool will be overweight at age 12.

Q: Won't children who have 'extra baby fat' as preschoolers slim down on their own as they grow?

A: Probably not, unless they change their eating habits and exercise regularly. Most children who are overweight in preschool will be overweight at age 12.

Q: The children I care for seem to always be on the move. Aren't young children already active enough?

A: Preschoolers may seem to always be on the move. Yet, most of their physical activity is really only sitting and squatting, lying down, standing, and walking (Brown et al., 2006). Today many young children are not as active as they need to be. They are also not as active as their parents were at this young age. They need to do more running, climbing, jumping and other large muscle activities to exercise their hearts and lungs.

Q: How can I help the children in my care?

A: Be sure the children in your care eat well and play hard. This simple phrase explains the best way to keep children fit and to avoid the many health problems that go with being overweight. There are three key ways to keep children from becoming overweight. Children need healthier foods in their diets. They need to spend less time sitting in front of screens. They also need lots of active play to prevent becoming obese.

So give the children in your care a healthy start in life. Let them have healthy foods in serving sizes that match their small bodies. Keep them from watching videos, DVDs, TV and computer screens while in your care. Give them the moderate to vigorous physical activity they need every day to stay fit and keep healthy. And help them learn the fundamental movement skills they need to stay active throughout their lives.

Q: Some of the mothers of overweight children in my care are obese themselves. How do I talk with these obese mothers about their children being overweight?

A: While most obese mothers see themselves as overweight, they do not see their overweight children as too heavy. Skip trying to convince parents that their preschoolers are overweight. Instead, talk to parents about helping their children develop a healthy lifestyle. Tell parents about the healthy food you serve and the active play that the children in your program enjoy every day. Keep the focus on healthy habits.

Young children who increase their physical activity levels show a decrease in body fat.

Q: I understand that children need moderate to vigorous physical activity daily. How can I tell if they are getting this?

A: When children are moderately to vigorously physically active, their hearts are beating faster and they are breathing harder than when they are just standing or walking slowly. They may also be a bit sweaty and slightly flushed. Walking quickly is moderate physical activity and running is vigorous physical activity.

Q: Why is daily moderate to vigorous physical activity so important for young children?

A: Here are some reasons why moderate to vigorous physical activity is so important.

• Young children who increase their physical activity levels show a decrease in body fat.

• Children get health benefits from moderate to vigorous physical activity. Daily physical activity reduces the likelihood that they will develop type 2 diabetes, cardiac problems, and other health concerns associated with being overweight. In the past, usually only adults had these health problems. Today these problems are more and more common in children who eat unhealthy food and do not get enough physical activity.

• Children learn to enjoy physical activity. They think of it as play, but they are practicing fundamental movement skills and improving their physical fitness at the same time. These happy experiences can lead to a lifetime interest in physical activity.

Q: How much physical activity do young children need?

A: The National Association of Sport and Physical Education (NASPE, 2002) says that preschoolers need:
- 60 minutes of structured physical activity, and
- 60 minutes of unstructured physical activity daily, and
- To not be sedentary for more than 60 minutes at a time,
    except when sleeping.

NASPE also recommends that children:
- Develop fundamental movement skills, and
- Have safe indoor and outdoor play areas, and
- Have caregivers who know the importance of physical activity and help children learn movement skills.

Lead children in structured physical activities every day.

Q: What does 'structured' and 'unstructured' physical activity mean?

A: *Unstructured physical activity* is the active play that children do when they are free to play on their own. This usually takes place outdoors in the yard or at the park, with toys and equipment that encourage them to play hard. Free play can be swinging and sliding on play equipment and climbing through a playhouse. It can be pushing and pulling toys, riding wheeled toys, and running around playing chase. In free play, the adult watches and encourages active play but does not lead the children's play.

Structured physical activity is different. It is activity for children that is planned and led by an adult. This book has 52 structured physical activities that are fun for children to play. Structured physical activities have clear goals for the children. They give children the chance to be moderately to vigorously active. They give children practice in fundamental movement skills and improve children's physical fitness. They can help children learn academic and social concepts, too. You can help children enjoy physical activity by giving them time for free play. Also lead them in structured physical activities every day.

Q: I regularly care for five children who are 9 months, 18 months, 2 years, 4 years and 5 years of age. After school an 11-year-old boy stays with us for two hours. How can I safely get all of these children doing structured physical activities together?

A: The physical activities in this book are made for young children of different ages to play together. Each activity has been child-tested and adult approved. We've led these activities in several family childcare settings with groups of three to twelve children. The children were 15 months to five years of age. We have also added ways for school-aged children to join in the fun. Real children of different ages, in real family childcare settings, have enjoyed playing these activities together.

Q: How can I fit so much physical activity into the childcare day?

A: Start simply. Plan a daily physical activity time. Begin with a warm-up. Add one activity from this book. Lead the children in it for up to 15 minutes. Choose a different activity to do the next day. Gradually add activities and increase the daily physical activity time to at least 30 minutes. Soon the children will be meeting the recommended NASPE standards. The 20-week curriculum in chapter 8 can help you get started.

The activities
in this book are
easy to lead.
Most need
little time
and equipment
to set up.

Q: I am not a physical educator. In fact, I hated physical education classes in school. How can I help young children learn movement skills?

A: The physical activities in this book have been tested with groups of young children in family childcare settings. They are easy to learn and fun for the children to do. They are easy to lead. Most need only inexpensive equipment. After a few weeks of doing structured physical activities, even the youngest children know the routines and look forward to the activities!

Q: I don't have a lot of room in my childcare setting. Can I do these physical activities in a small space?

A: Most of the activities work well both outdoors and indoors. Many of these activities have been done, with great success, in the living room of a city apartment. These activities are perfect for those rainy days when the children need to be active but are confined to a small indoor space.

Q: I'm careful about how I spend money on toys and equipment. Does the equipment for these activities cost a lot of money?

A: No, these physical activities use only inexpensive items. You might already have them in your home. If not, they are for sale at discount and dollar stores. Only things like laundry baskets, rolled socks, and punch ball balloons covered with pantyhose are needed. Balled newspapers, plastic plates or Frisbees, pool noodles, bubble wrap, carpet squares, game cards and hula hoops are also used.

Q: I don't have a lot of extra time for setting up and cleaning up after physical activities. Can I do these activities without spending a lot of extra time?

A: These activities are easy to lead. Most need little time and equipment to set up. Once you have taught the activities to the children, many of the activities run themselves. They require supervision but not much adult direction.

Promote a healthy lifestyle on behalf of the children in your care! Make sure they eat well and play hard.

Q: Some of my children are very coordinated. They are much more skilled than others their age. One child has a physical disability and has difficulty moving. Will these children find the activities too easy or too difficult?

A: We give ways to make activities easier or harder. You can change each activity to match the skill level of each child. We also give ways to include preschoolers with special needs. These ideas are for children with developmental delays, physical disabilities, or blindness.

You have an important role in preparing young children in your care to succeed in school and in life. Help these children learn to eat healthy foods and enjoy daily physical activity. They will also be learning how to avoid obesity, even as they become adults. What you do on their behalf will make a major contribution to their future health! So start now. Promote a healthy lifestyle on behalf of the children in your care! Make sure they eat well and play hard!

Remember:
- Obesity in young children is a significant problem.
- Overweight children can develop type 2 diabetes, high blood pressure and other diseases normally seen in much older people.
- Most children who are overweight in preschool will be overweight at 12 years of age.
- Children who eat well and play hard benefit from better health, lower body fat, better fitness and more self-esteem.
- NASPE recommends preschool children have 60 minutes of structured and 60 minutes of unstructured physical activity each day.
- Adults in charge of children need to give them nutritious food and many opportunities for vigorous play.

The next chapter explains what children can learn while enjoying physical activity.

Learning
through Physical Activity

2

As children
are physically
active, they
are learning
fundamental
movement
skills.

They are
learning about
their feelings.

They are
learning about
the world
around them.

In the previous chapter we focused on the health benefits of physical activities for children. In this chapter we'll look beyond health benefits to consider what children can learn while doing physical activities. Consider this: "Children are doing more than just moving when playing games and activities. As they play, they are feeling, thinking and moving all at the same time. Through these movement experiences they are changing their behaviors. They are learning!" (McCall and Craft, 2000, p. 10)

Q: What can toddlers and preschoolers learn through structured physical activities?

A: Toddlers and preschool children can learn many things doing the structured physical activities in this book. Here is a brief summary of some of the skills and concepts they can learn, from McCall and Craft (2000).

As children are physically active, they are learning fundamental movement skills.
They are practicing how to do fundamental movement skills. They are learning to run, jump, throw, kick, twist and turn. They are also improving their physical fitness.

As children are physically active, they are learning about their feelings.
They are deciding how they feel about themselves and the way that they move. They are deciding whether they like being physically active. They are deciding whether they want to continue being active on their own. They are learning how to get along with others, including learning to share and take turns. They are deciding whether they enjoy and can be successful in physical activities.

As children are physically active, they are learning about the world around them.
They are learning important cognitive concepts that will lay the foundation for academic achievement in school. They are learning to follow instructions and simple rules of the games. They are learning the names of their body parts and how their bodies move. They are also learning about objects, colors, and shapes so they can recognize and name them. They are learning basic movement concepts, with special emphasis on learning spatial relationships. And, they are also learning about eating foods that will help keep their bodies healthy

A complete description of what we want young children to learn through physical activity, known as curricular goals, is in chapter two of the McCall and Craft book titled *Moving with a Purpose: Developing Programs for Preschoolers of All Abilities.*

> The process through which our bodies learn to move is called motor development. It is a fascinating study!

Seven of the most important goals that physical activities can help young children achieve are listed below, and also along the top of the Game Finder on page vi in this book.

- Learn object, color, shape recognition
- Learn spatial relationships
- Learn locomotor skills
- Learn object control skills
- Learn stability
- Develop cardiovascular endurance
- Develop muscular strength and endurance

This chapter discusses what is meant by each of these curricular goals. It also lists physical activities that can help children achieve them. First, we explain the fundamental movement phase of motor development and its three parts: locomotor, object control, and stability. Next, we talk about physical fitness, including the components cardiovascular endurance and muscular strength and endurance. Then we share ideas for using physical activities to teach cognitive concepts, especially object, color, shape recognition, and spatial relationships. Finally, we explore ways to use physical activities to teach about healthy foods.

Learning Fundamental Movement Skills

How can a newborn, who has not yet learned to hold up his head, develop into an adult who can swish a basket from 30 feet away? How can a toddler, who can barely walk, develop into a teenager who can do a back flip on a balance beam? How can a preschooler, who can hardly stand on one foot, perform a triple axel while figure skating as an adult? The process through which our bodies learn to move is called motor development. It is a fascinating study! This section looks at how we humans learn to move.

Children go through four phases of motor development as they grow and improve their movement skills. Each phase lays the foundation for progress in the next one.

- For the first few months of life, infants are in the *Reflexive Movement Phase.*
- As they learn to roll over, sit up, pick up and let go of objects, pull to a stand and take their first steps, they are in the *Rudimentary Movement Phase.*
- The following phase, the *Fundamental Movement Phase,* begins around age two. This phase continues for the next several years. Children build on their walking skills to learn to run, jump, hop, slide, gallop, skip and leap. They learn to throw, catch, kick, and strike, as well. Also, they learn to twist, turn, bend, stretch, swing, roll and balance their bodies.

Generally, the more skilled children are in the fundamental movement skills, the more successful they will be in sport and active recreation.

- The fourth phase of motor development begins around age seven. It then continues throughout life. It is called the *Specialized Movement Phase.* People refine their fundamental movement skills to play sports and active recreation.

Q: What are fundamental movement skills?

A: A skill is the ability to do something well. Usually lots of practice is needed to develop a skill. Fundamental movement skills are basic human movements developed through practice. These skills are organized into three categories.

- *Locomotor skills* are movements we use to move from place to place. Running, jumping, hopping, sliding, galloping, skipping and leaping are all locomotor skills.

- *Object control skills* are the movements we use to swing a bat, catch a ball, and use other objects in a controlled manner. Throwing, catching, kicking and striking are all object control skills.

- *Stability movements* are the skills that help us keep our balance while changing body position. Twisting, turning, bending, stretching, swinging, springing, balancing while upright and upside down, are all stability movements.

These are the fundamental movement skills.

Locomotor Skills	Object Control	Stability Skills
Walking	Throwing	Turning
Running	Catching	Twisting
Jumping	Kicking	Bending
Hopping	Striking	Stretching
Galloping	Trapping	Reaching
Sliding	Dribbling	Lifting
Skipping	Ball rolling	Falling
Leaping	Volleying	

Q: Why is it so important for children to learn and practice fundamental movement skills?

A: Everyone needs mature fundamental movement skills! Dancing and long distance running and golf and virtually all lifetime physical activities depend on mature fundamental movement skills.

Generally, the more skilled children are in the fundamental movement skills, the more successful they will be in sport and active recreation. Many of the physical activities in this book can help children practice their fundamental movement skills.

Children learn
that moving
and being
physically active
is easy and fun,
and can be
enjoyed
over a lifetime.

Q: What cues can I say to help the children learn how to do each fundamental movement skill?

A: Look at the following physical activities in chapter 4 for cues to help children learn these fundamental movement skills:

Run – **Running with Streamers**
Jump – **Bubble Wrap Jumping** and **On/Off**
Hop – **Hoop Scotch**
Gallop – **Puzzle Carry**
Throw – **Clean Out the Backyard: Throwing**
Catch – **Easy Catching**
Kick – **Clean Out the Backyard: Kicking**
Strike – **Easy Striking**

Q: Is there another reason for the children in my care to practice these skills?

A: Yes. Children with lots of practice in fundamental movement skills before they begin kindergarten can have an advantage over others. These children are likely to be more confident and successful in physical activities.[1] Even more importantly, children who have mature fundamental movement skills are more likely to choose to be physically active into their teenage years. Because they are remaining physically active, they are less likely to become overweight or obese. It is extremely important that children learn that moving and being physically active is easy and fun, and can be enjoyed over a lifetime. This all starts in their preschool years.

Q: Will every child I care for be able to learn these movement skills?

A: Infants and young toddlers in childcare settings are usually not yet ready to learn fundamental movement skills. They are still in the rudimentary movement phase.

Most two- to five-year-olds have reached the fundamental movement phase. These children can usually do the activities in this book, but at their own level. Less-skilled children might walk fast, instead of run. They might need their hands held to help with balance. During matching activities, some might be able to carry items but not know how to find their mates. The important things are that the children practice their skills, play hard, and have fun doing the activity!

Preschoolers with developmental delays may need extra time and practice to learn to sit, stand, and take their first steps. Spina bifida, cerebral palsy, amputation, and other orthopedic impairments may limit some children's movements. Their best way to move might be very different from the way other children move. Help find a way of moving that works best for each child based on his or her unique body.

Children need to be physically fit to enjoy active play.

In addition to providing practice of the fundamental movement skills, physical activities can also help children become physically fit.

Developing Physical Fitness

Children need to be physically fit to enjoy active play. If a child's fitness level is so low that she is always out of breath when she plays, she may not enjoy being physically active. If a child's muscles are screaming for oxygen when he runs, he may try to avoid physical activity. As children are active in their play, they also become physically fit.

Physical fitness means that the heart, blood vessels, lungs, and muscles are all working efficiently. Physical fitness includes cardiovascular endurance, muscular strength and endurance, and flexibility. The following section explains each of these terms.

Q: What is cardiovascular endurance? How do children develop it?

A. *Cardiovascular endurance* is the ability of the heart, lungs, and circulatory system systems to work efficiently. Many adults run, swim, or cycle to develop their cardiovascular endurance. Fortunately, young children do not need to do boring exercises to get fit. All most children need to do to develop their cardiovascular endurance is to play hard. This approach to fitness is fun! Many physical activities in this book can help children develop cardiovascular endurance. A few examples are **All Stop & Go to Music**, **Bubble Wrap Jumping**, **Running with Streamers**, and **Swat the Fly**.

Q: What are muscular strength and muscular endurance? How can children develop them?

A: *Muscular strength* is how much work a muscle can do only one time. It is muscular strength that is needed to pick up a very heavy box only one time. *Muscular endurance* is how much work a muscle can do again and again. Muscular endurance is needed to pick up a heavy box over and over. Children can develop muscular strength and muscular endurance through active play. Lead a variety of physical activities so children have to use all of their muscles.

Many children have weak upper bodies. One way for children to develop their upper body strength is to lift their body weight with their arms. Another way is to push, pull and support objects. Playing on the monkey bars, horizontal bars, climbing ladders and jungle gyms are fun ways for children to build upper body strength. Physical activities in this book that can help children develop upper body muscular strength and endurance include **Frog Catcher**, **Lug-a-Jug**, **Paper Plate Scooters**, and **Push & Pull Baskets**. One caution: If a child is very overweight, change the activity so he is only lifting part of his body weight.

Obtain advice from the child's medical professional before involving a child with known health concerns in physical activity.

Q: What is flexibility? Do most young children need to develop it?

A. *Flexibility* means a joint can move through its full range of motion. This book does not provide flexibility activities. Most young children are already very flexible. This is not the case for children with spastic cerebral palsy or some other disabilities. Ask physical or occupational therapists for ways to help increase these children's flexibility.

Q: Will children feel uncomfortable when they are very active?

A: Use daily physical activity time to help children learn how their bodies feel when they are very active. Help children learn that those feelings mean that they are doing things that are healthy and good for their bodies. Here are a few cues for children:

- You have been running a long time. Feel your heart beat fast. That is good for your body. You are exercising your heart and making your heart stronger.
- When you sweat and breathe hard while you are physically active, it is good. It means that you are giving your body a healthy workout.
- You ran all the way across the yard without stopping. That is good!
- You traveled far on the monkey bars. You are making your body stronger.
- It is fine to feel tired after: running so far, or running so fast, or jumping so long, or using your arms to carry that heavy weight. It means that you are giving your body a healthy workout.

Obtain advice from the child's medical professional before involving a child with known health concerns in physical activity. Be alert for and report to family adults any symptoms that may indicate cardiac conditions, exercise-induced asthma attacks, or other health concerns. Watch for bluish lips and nail beds during vigorous activity. These might be signs of cardiac problems. Watch for prolonged shortness of breath, difficulty exhaling or wheezing. These might indicate an asthma attack.

Now we know that physical activities can help children learn fundamental movement skills and develop physical fitness. This next section presents ways to use physical activities to help young children learn cognitive concepts.

Exercise creates the "environment in which the brain is ready, willing, and able to learn."[2]

Learning Cognitive Concepts

There is a clear link between movement and learning. Jean Piaget noted that very young children's primary way of learning is through movement. Just watch the actions of a one-year-old who has begun to walk. He toddles, finds a toy, picks it up, explores it with his hands and mouth, loses interest, and drops it. He then toddles to the next toy, picks it up, feels it with his hands and mouth, loses interest, and drops it. He is learning through movement.

Brain research shows that children learn well when they are active. Moderate exercise improves thinking and increases the number of brain cells. During movement, children use several senses together, creating new connecting pathways in the brain. Exercise creates the "environment in which the brain is ready, willing, and able to learn."[2]

Q: I don't have time for a daily physical activity time. Isn't it more important to use that time to teach the academic concepts children will need to succeed in school?

A: Childcare providers do not need to make a choice between physical activity and academic learning. Academic concepts can be taught *through* physical activity.[3]

Q: What academic concepts can young children learn through physical activities?

A: Fun physical activities can be used to help children learn to recognize objects, colors, shapes, letters and numbers. All of these concepts can be taught through what we call Carry Games. In these games, children carry objects to match with other objects as they move from one end of the play area to the other and back. Carry Games in this book that practice object, color, or shape recognition include **Color Challenge**, **Go Fishing**, **Matching Numbers**, **Matching Socks**, **Puzzle Carry**, and **Rainbow Pieces**.

Physical activities are also great for teaching spatial relationships. This means knowing where one object is in relation to another. Some words that describe spatial relationships are: under, over, around, through, above, below, next to, between, and inside. Children who do not know these basic spatial relationship words may have a hard time understanding what they are told to do when in school. "Put your book inside your desk." "Store your boots under the shelf." "Print your name at the top of the page." Each of these statements can be confusing for children who don't know the meaning of these words.

Children
who have had
fun playing
with pictures of
foods might be
willing to try
the new foods.

Give the children in your care a real head start in school by leading physical activities that teach these spatial relationships. Play **Feed the Penguins, On/Off, Garden Friends,** and **Obstacle Course: Outdoor, Obstacle Course: Indoor,** and **Obstacle Course: Under, Over, Through**. As you play these activities, talk with the children about where they are in relation to objects around them.

Physical activities can help children learn cognitive concepts. They can also help children learn about eating healthy foods.

Learning to Try Healthy Foods

Q: Some of the children in my care will only eat a few foods. They won't even try other foods. Can I use physical activities to introduce them to new, healthy foods?

A: Children are often told, "Don't play with your food!" In some of this book's physical activities, we try to get children to 'play' with healthy foods that might be new to them. These activities use pictures of foods, not the real food. In **Healthy Food Hunting** children move across the room or yard to match pictures of fruits and vegetables on cards. In **Jump & Shop** they pretend to shop for healthy foods, jumping around the room gathering and placing cards of fruits or vegetables in their shopping bags. In **Stocking Grocery Shelves**, they are doing the reverse of shopping. The children restock the shelves of their pretend grocery store with picture cards of fruits and vegetables. Children who have had fun playing with pictures of these foods might be willing to try the new foods. Ideally, serve the children one of these foods right after playing a game that included the food. It may take several exposures to a new food before a child will accept its taste, so these games are a start.

Remember:

• Young children are learning how to move and how they feel about moving when they are playing physical activities.
• Children can learn cognitive concepts while having fun playing physical activities.
• Most two- to six-year-olds are in the fundamental movement phase of motor development.
• During the fundamental movement phase children learn locomotor skills, object control skills, and stability movements.
• Mastery of fundamental movement skills is the foundation for learning the specialized movement skills needed to enjoy a lifetime of sport and recreational activities.
• Children who enter kindergarten with nearly mature fundamental movement skills are likely to be more confident and successful in physical activities than their classmates who lack these skills.
• Playing hard helps children develop cardiovascular endurance and muscle strength and endurance.

Children can learn so many movement skills and cognitive concepts through doing physical activities. The next chapter tells how to lead these activities so children can get the benefits.

---

1 "Failure to develop and refine fundamental and specialized movement skills during the crucial preschool and elementary school years often leads children to frustration and failure during adolescence and adulthood. ...Children cannot take part, with success, in an activity if they have not learned the essential movement skills contained within the activity" (Gallahue, 1996, p. 36).

"Children have the developmental potential to be at the mature stage of most fundamental movement skills by about age six" (Gallahue & Ozmun, 2002, p. 182). But it is only through many, many, many opportunities to practice these skills during the preschool years that a child is likely to realize this potential.

2 Early childhood educators have long known, through observation, that most children learn well when they are active. Now recent brain research has strengthened the notion that learning benefits from movement. "Strong evidence supports the connection between movement and learning. Evidence from imaging sources, anatomical studies, and clinical data shows that moderate exercise enhances cognitive processing. It also increases the number of brain cells" (Jensen, 2005, p. 67). "Early childhood educators have become increasingly aware that movement plays an important role in the future development of a young child. During movement activities children use multiple sensory modalities, thereby creating neural connections across numerous pathways in the brain" (National Association for Sport and Physical Education, 2000, p. 2). "Physical activity sparks biological changes that encourage brain cells to bind to one another. For brains to learn, these connections must be made" (Ratey, 2008, p. 10). Neuroscientists studying the brain confirm "exercise provides an unparalleled stimulus, creating an environment in which the brain is ready, willing, and able to learn" (Ratey, 2008, p. 10).

3 "Young children learn and develop in an integrated fashion. Motor, cognitive, emotional, and social development are interrelated" (National Association for Sport and Physical Education, 2000, p. 7). Movement and academic concepts can, and should, be taught together.

Leading
Physical Activities

3

The key
is to make
being active
fun for the
children.

Chapter 1 discussed the need young children have for nutritious food and vigorous physical activity. Chapter 2 talked about the importance of mastering fundamental movement skills and what children learn about themselves and the world through vigorous play. This chapter explores ways to successfully plan for and give children in your care the vigorous physical activity experiences they need to stay fit and healthy.

Childcare providers sometimes say, "I was never any good in physical education classes. I have no idea how to lead physical activities with young children." If you are not sure of your skill in getting children up and moving, relax! If you just make the physical activities fun, the children will love doing them. And, you'll look like you have been leading children in physical activities for a long time!

Q: How can I make physical activities interesting for children?

A: There are several simple yet important ways you help children enjoy physical activities. We discuss each in detail below. At this point it is important to know that you can be successful leading children in active play. The key is to make being active fun for the children. Preschoolers like doing the activities in this book because they were made just them. They will also like the physical activities you come up with, as long as they are having fun!

Q: Why do these physical activities have to be fun for the children?

A: Have you ever heard someone make a comment about an adult who was having so much fun he was acting like a little kid? Fun is what motivates children. Fun is what life is all about for kids. An activity that appears to be fun, because some children are enjoying it, will seem very attractive to other children and draw them in like a magnet. So *invite* children to do physical activities. Make sure they are fun activities to do. Some children will love the activities at once. Others will see the fun those children are having and will quickly join you.

Q: I think physical activities are usually hard work. How can they be fun for the children?

A: Physical activities can be hard work for children, but children will do the hard work if they are motivated. The best way to motivate children is to give them a reason for doing the activity. A well-designed physical activity, with a purpose the children see as reasonable, can be so much fun that children will ignore how hard their bodies are working. They will just think about the great time they are having.

Every activity in this book is designed to have a fun purpose the children will understand and that will motivate them to do the activity.

The first few times we led young children in Swat the Fly, we weren't prepared for how excited the children became and how hard they ran. The activity was simple – one child pulled a 'fly' along the ground, and others chased the fly and tried to swat it with a foam pool noodle. Children loved the chase, they loved catching the fly, and they really loved swatting it as they ran. And the children pulling the fly worked extra hard trying to run fast enough to escape the swatters. All because they were having FUN!

Q: Please explain what you mean by 'give the activities a purpose.'

A: Activities in this book are designed with several purposes in mind. Most have the purpose of developing children's fundamental movement skills and physical fitness. Many are also designed to give the children practice with academic concepts. These are some of the purposes we adults see as important in the activities. But the children need to decide that the activity is interesting to them before they will want to do it. For this reason, every activity in this book is designed to have a fun purpose the children will understand and that will motivate them to do the activity.

Take our experience asking children to walk on a flat foam pool noodle lying on the floor. We wanted them to walk on the pool noodle to develop their stability. We knew the children would do it four or five times in a row before becoming bored. So instead of asking them to just walk on the flat pool noodle, we gave the activity a purpose we thought the children might enjoy. We told them the noodle was really a bridge over a swamp where a hungry alligator lived. The children had to walk over the bridge and carry things to a basket on the other side. On each trip they had to pass a hungry, watchful alligator. On each trip the load the children had to carry became more difficult for them. The alligator chased any children who dropped something or stepped off the bridge into the swamp! So with a little imagination, walking on the pool noodle to practice stability became the thrilling game **Alligator Pit**! In the children's eyes, the stability activity had a fun purpose that made it worth doing over and over again.

Q: What activity 'purposes' do children like the best?

A: Preschool children like activities that let them show how strong or fast or clever they are. Preschoolers also tend to enjoy activities that let them pretend to do adults' tasks and use things that adults use. **Running with Streamers** lets children play with crepe paper streamers. This can be exciting because they may have only seen streamers as party decorations that they were not allowed to touch.

Try to change activities so that each child, regardless of ability, can be successful at least three out of four tries.

Laundry Pick-Up and **Stocking Grocery Shelves** let children pretend to do adult jobs. **Push & Pull Baskets** lets children have fun in the same laundry basket adults use to do the laundry. **Lug-a-Jug** lets children play with the large, heavy jugs adults use to store water or milk. Both **Push & Pull Baskets** and **Lug-a-Jug** give children chances to proudly show everyone how strong they are!

Q: Is giving each activity a 'purpose' all that is needed to get children active?

A: Getting children interested in doing physical activities is just the first step. Keeping them interested is the next step. Children enjoy doing fun things. However, the fun can quickly disappear from an activity if it is too easy or too hard. Being successful in a challenging activity is key to children's enjoyment of it.

Q: Can children who have different abilities be successful in the same physical activity?

A: Most children can be successful in the same physical activities, regardless of age or abilities, if the activities are designed to accommodate a wide range of abilities. One key for success is to discourage competition and comparisons among children. Simply refuse to compare children with each other. Another key is to set up activities that encourage participation at any ability level. The physical activities in this book are made so that young children, regardless of age or skill or special needs, can play at a level that matches their ages and abilities.

Most of the activities in this book include ways to make them easier and harder. Some activities have tips for modifying equipment, too. Try to change activities so that each child, regardless of ability, can be successful at least three out of four tries. This means increasing the challenge for more-skilled children, and finding ways to make it easier for less-skilled children.

Let's look at how children of different skill levels can all be included in a throwing activity. Children who are just learning how to grasp and release a ball can be held over a target and 'throw' by simply dropping the ball onto the target. For children who can stand and throw, make a barrier that children have to stay behind while throwing at the target. Angle the barrier so it is closer to the target at one end and farther away at the other. Beginning throwers can stand close to the target at one end of the barrier. Experienced throwers can stand farther away from the target at the other end. In this way, all children can play together and be challenged, still hitting the target most of the time.

Eliminate elimination games!

Q: Are there other ways to promote the success of children doing physical activities?

A: Yes. Give children lots of encouragement to inspire their success. Congratulate them when they try new activities and work toward becoming skillful movers. Resist saying negative things such as, "Don't do it that way," and "That's wrong." Keep positive remarks flowing in a ratio of four positive comments for every constructively critical comment. Give specific positive comments to inspire children, such as "Great job! You stepped forward as you threw." "Nice work looking at the ball as you kicked it." "My, you are moving fast!" "That's really heavy. You must be strong to move that." Also give constructive comments, such as "Try moving closer to the target when you throw." "Bring the ball back by your ear before you throw."

Another great way to promote success is to eliminate elimination games! In elimination games the least-skilled children are usually eliminated first. Yet they are the children who need the most practice. Elimination games also keep many children from being active, requiring them to just sit and watch the rest of the game. Being eliminated quickly takes the fun out of an activity. It is often embarrassing, too. Only one child wins in an elimination game. Everyone else is a loser! Our objective in this book is to provide activities that have children up and moving during the entire activity, not sitting on the side as losers!

Q: How can children play elimination games such as Musical Chairs, without having to be eliminated?

A: Think about how you might substitute participation for elimination in activities. **Musical Hoops**, for instance, is a well-known modification of the elimination game Musical Chairs. While the music plays, children run around the outside of the hula hoops placed on the floor. As soon as the music stops, they must find and stand inside a hoop. So far, the activity is just like musical chairs. But now we take away one hoop each time the music restarts. The activity becomes a cooperative activity. Hoops, not children, are eliminated. The next time the music stops, all the children have fewer hoops to stand in. They must share the remaining hoops with other children. At the end of the activity, all of the children, to their delight, share just one hoop!

The following activities in this book are all elimination games that have been changed to continuous participation games: **All Stop & Go to Music, Alligator Pit, Frog Catcher, Hoop Limbo, Hoop Scotch, Land/Lake, On/Off,** and **Spiders & Bugs.**

> Encourage
> children
> to explore and
> experiment
> with movement
> in safe
> and fun ways.

Q: Sometimes the toddlers in my group don't follow the instructions. They tend to change the way the activities are done. Is this okay?

A: Most toddlers can do the activities in this book if there are a few older, preschool children for them to copy. Many of the activities in this book would be difficult to do with only toddlers in the group. Toddlers are just becoming aware that there are different ways to do things. They constantly experiment to find what suits them best. Sometimes when you instruct the children to run, one or two children will walk instead. Or when you ask them to pick up one puzzle piece, some will grab a handful. Encourage the children to do as you ask. Also give them chances to try something different on their own. It could be they did not listen to the instructions. Or perhaps they wanted to do something they saw another child doing. If there is not a safety or behavior issue, don't stop the activity because the child did something a little differently. Instead, keep the activity going while you quietly give feedback to just that one child. Try to give the children as many choices as possible when doing this book's physical activities. Encourage children to explore and experiment with movement in safe and fun ways.

Some children will take longer than others to finish tasks. Don't make the quicker children wait for the others. When faster children return from doing tasks in Carry Games, immediately give them another card to carry. Don't make them stop and wait for others to catch up. Keep the flow of the activity going for all children at their own ability levels.

Q: Some children in my group get bored easily with the same activities. How can I keep them interested?

A: Plan to keep your physical activity time fresh. Have lots of activities from which to choose. Add at least one new physical activity a week to your program. Also, give children ample free play at other times during the day.

Avoid doing the same activity until children become bored. Try to switch physical activities just after the peak of excitement. Use a kitchen timer to remind you to change the activity after about 15 minutes. This will keep the children eager to play it again on another day

Q: Will the children, regardless of age, be able to do a single physical activity for 15 minutes?

A: Young children have short attention spans. Keep instructions to less than two minutes. The youngest children are likely to lose interest in an activity before others. Be prepared to keep them occupied with an extra brief task such as sorting objects. This will give the older children time to finish the physical activity.

Children with developmental delays can often be included by doing the suggestions under the heading *Easier* in each physical activity.

Including Children with Special Needs

Q: I have a child with a developmental delay in my program. How can I include her in these physical activities?

A: A developmental delay is when a child's behavior, language, learning, social or physical skills are far behind those of other children of the same age. Children with intellectual disabilities, cerebral palsy, autism, and many other disabilities may have developmental delays. This book's physical activities list ideas for making the activity easier for younger children. Children with developmental delays can often be included by doing the suggestions under the heading *Easier* in each physical activity presented in chapter 4. You may want to ask the children to walk or run instead of the harder skills of jump, hop, or gallop.

Children with developmental delays have behaviors, understanding and language typical of children who are younger. They are also likely to have motor skills typical of younger children. Most preschoolers are ready to practice their fundamental movement skills. Yet, three- four-and five-year-olds with significant developmental delays might still need practice with rudimentary movement skills. They may need more practice learning to sit, stand and take their first steps. These are skills typically practiced by six- to fifteen-month-olds. Refer to chapter 5 for physical activities that might be right for preschoolers with developmental delays who need practice with rudimentary movement skills.

Q: A child in my care seems highly distractible. He flits from task to task, but never completes anything. How can I help this child pay attention long enough to do the physical activity with the rest of us?

A: The same techniques that you use to lead physical activities with other preschoolers may become essential in leading children who are highly distractible. These ways are described later in this chapter. Use floor spots, clear 'go' and 'stop' cues, and short directions. Also give a reminder cue just before the child is to act. Give lots of positive feedback for what the child is doing well. You may also wish to hold a distractible child's hand during physical activities to help keep the child focused on the task.

Q: What about the children who use wheelchairs or mobile prone standers, or are pushed in strollers to get from place to place? How can children with physical disabilities do these physical activities if they cannot walk on their own?

A: The physical activities in this book can be changed. You may want to shorten or eliminate the distance that a child who cannot walk needs to travel. Position children with limited mobility close to the targets in throwing activities. Also place the objects to throw within their easy reach. You can also ask other children to hand them the objects.

> In teaching children with autism, use as much structure and routine as you can in your physical activity time.

In Carry Games children who are unable to walk due to a physical impairment may move in other ways. They may be able to roll, scoot, or drag, or use a wheeled toy such as a big wheel toy to get from place the place. Shorten the distance the children are to travel to make moving a challenge but not an impossible one.

Q: One year I cared for a child who was blind. How can these activities be adapted so that this child could join them?

A: Physical activities are very important for children with visual impairments. This is because these children tend to stay in one place much of the day. They need to get out and learn how to explore what is around them. Learn how to guide a child who is blind, by allowing the child to hold your hand as you walk. Also encourage the child to follow the sound of your voice without actually touching you. Use toys with sounds such as rattles and balls with bells inside to stimulate a child who is blind to move toward the sound.

Q: And how do I include a child who is deaf?

A: The challenge is to find a way to communicate that does not depend on hearing. Learn what means of communication the child is being taught and then learn it yourself. This often means learning basic signs in American Sign Language. Use these signs as you are talking to the hearing children so the deaf child is also part of the conversation. Give many demonstrations to help the child understand what you would like her to do.

Other ways to include children with special needs are found in the physical activities throughout chapter 4.

Q: There is a child with autism in my care. Is there anything special that I can do to help him join in the physical activities?

A: So much depends on the unique characteristics of each child with autism. Children with autism often want things to be exactly the same in their daily routines. In teaching children with autism, use as much structure and routine as you can in your physical activity time. Plan that the child will have his own floor spot on the same place in the room every time. Stopping one activity and beginning the next one can also be a difficult time. Give a countdown for transitions to help the child anticipate what is going to happen next. Use statements such as, "In three more turns we're going to put away the balls and bring out the hula hoops… Now in two more turns… In one more turn… Now we are going to play with the hoops." Learn whether the child is receiving services from a speech therapist. If so, ask this person to show you how to use the Picture Exchange Communication System (PECS). These picture cards give a pre-school child who is not speaking a way to communicate.

If at any point an activity becomes unsafe, stop it immediately.

Leading Physical Activity Time

Q: How do I lead the physical activity time?

A: The first step is to be organized. Routines are essential to working with young children. Just as you and the children have routines for beginning and ending the day, mealtime, snack time, naptime, and playtime, have routines prepared for leading physical activity time. Build a set time for structured physical activity into the childcare day. Use a set schedule to help the children adjust to having structured physical activity every day.

1. **Have a clear beginning to the physical activity time.** Gather the children together and have each child sit on his or her own floor spot or carpet square. This helps organize your space and gives each child a home base to which to return. It also helps the children understand their job is to listen to what you say when they are sitting on their floor spots.

2. **Have clear boundaries**. Boundaries show children where they can and cannot go during the activity. Most young children do not understand complex concepts such as 'stand behind the line.' Use physical barriers as boundaries to keep children safely away from danger. Ideas on making effective barriers are offered at the end of this chapter.

3. **Briefly explain and demonstrate the activity.** Have the children sitting on their floor spots as you do this. Keep your explanation short, only one to two minutes in length. Then show the children what you want them to do.

4. **Use recorded music as a signal to start and stop physical activities.** Explain to the children, "When the music starts, you may start moving. When the music stops, you are to stop where you are and listen for instructions." **All Stop & Go to Music** and **Musical Hoops** are activities that help children practice listening to musical cues.

5. During the physical activity, **give plenty of verbal cues, encouragement and constructive corrections to the children.** Try to give children four encouraging comments for every one constructive correction

6. **If at any point an activity becomes unsafe, stop it immediately.** Turn off the music. Have the children return to their floor spots. Refocus the children. Re-explain or change the activity as needed, and begin again.

7. **Make clear, easily recognized transitions** between physical activities. When using music, turn it off as a cue for the children to stop. Ask them to return to their floor spots and sit down. Briefly explain the next activity. Invite the children to stand up and get ready as you restart the music.

The activities
in this book
require you
to watch
the children
as they
do each one.

8. **Provide closure at the end** of the structured physical activity time. Turn off the music. Have the children sit on their floor spots. Talk about the activity. Ask the children how they felt doing the activity. Explain how the activity helped to make them healthier. Then sing a closing song together just before ending physical activity time.

9. **Ask the children to help collect any equipment** used during the activity. Have them bring it to you for storage.

10. **Have water**, not soda or fruit juice, available for children to drink during and after the physical activity time.

Health, Safety and Equipment Considerations

Q: Are there any health concerns about leading physical activities with children? If so, what are they?

A: Learn whether there are any health concerns that might limit a child's physical activity. Discuss the health of each child in your care with the parents. Review each child's health records. Learn whether it is not a good idea for a child to do any specific physical activity.

Get advice from the child's medical professional for any child who is known to have health problems. Cardiac conditions, exercise-induced asthma, or sickle cell anemia are examples of conditions that might limit children's physical activity. Watch for bluish lips and nail beds during vigorous activity. This might be a sign of cardiac problems. Watch for prolonged shortness of breath, difficulty exhaling, or wheezing. This might indicate an asthma attack. Stop any child from participating in an activity if you see these symptoms, or other health or safety concerns. Tell the parent what you saw as soon as possible.

Ask the advice of the child's physical or occupational therapist about positioning and mobility recommendations for any child with cerebral palsy or other orthopedic condition in your care.

Q: What safety concerns are there when leading physical activities with children?

A: Children can be creative and quick in the ways they can place themselves in danger. The activities in this book require you to watch the children as they do each one.

We cannot anticipate all possible safety concerns in leading physical activities. Here are some of the more important safety issues to think about when doing physical activities with children. All of these activities require that you use sound judgment in planning and leading physical activities with young children.

> Have all preschoolers run in the same direction so they don't run into each other.

Watch the children at all times during physical activities

It is key that you always watch the children. Watch for changes in a child's activity level that might indicate a health issue. Watch children for safe behavior. Use your own good judgment in anticipating and preventing anything that might be unsafe for the children.

Help children develop their listening skills

Children need to listen and act quickly when you give safety instructions. **All Stop & Go to Music** and **On/Off** both give children practice listening and responding to verbal cues. Start physical activity time with one of these activities to build children's listening skills.

Running

Most preschool children are not yet skilled in dodging objects while running. Have all preschoolers run in the same direction so they don't run into each other. In contrast, school-aged children can usually dodge each other, such as is required in the popular game Freeze Tag. Never ask children to run to a wall or fence or any other immovable object. Most young children cannot yet judge distances or stop quickly. Children are likely to run full speed into the wall. Make the boundary several feet in front of any wall or other immovable object in case children run past the stopping point. This gives the children extra space in which to stop.

There may also be times and places where running might be impractical or unsafe for children. In these cases, substitute other locomotor skills such as jumping and hopping.

Older children playing with younger children

Be sure that larger, heavier children do not roughhouse with smaller, lighter children. A heavier child falling on a small child can cause injury. When larger and smaller children play together, do activities that don't require body contact. The activities in this book have been done successfully in settings with multi-age groups of children. However, you will need to decide whether the activities will work safely for the children in your care. If the activity seems unsafe for any child, do not play it.

Be careful when children are kicking or throwing objects toward each other. Use only lightweight balls for kicking and soft fluff balls, sponge balls, or rolled socks for throwing.

Q: What equipment should I get first?

A: Getting young children to sit in their own space while you briefly explain activities can be a challenge. Have one carpet square or floor spot for each child to sit on every time you give instructions during physical activity time. Sports equipment companies sell floor spots, called poly spots. Carpet remnants can be cut into carpet squares. Floor spots or carpet squares are also needed for the **Obstacle Courses**, and the activities **Frog Catcher**, **On/Off** and **Land/Lake**. In addition, they can be used to mark activity play areas.

As soon as you can, start collecting pairs of children's socks. Parents may have clean, used pairs to donate. Buy hula hoops, foam pool noodles, sturdy and flexible plastic plates, punch ball or helium quality balloons, and pairs of pantyhose. These items are often sold in dollar stores. Check each activity's equipment list to see what else you will need. Test all items for safety before letting children play with them.

Kicking, throwing, and striking activities

Be careful when children are kicking or throwing objects toward each other, as in the two **Clean Out the Backyard** activities. Use only lightweight balls for kicking and soft fluff balls, sponge balls, or rolled socks for throwing. Also, watch the kicking and throwing skills of the children. Are there children who can kick or throw hard enough that the ball would hurt another child, if struck? If so, do not let them kick or throw in the direction of other children. Provide a different kicking or throwing activity for these skilled children. The same caution applies to striking. Use only foam pool noodles as bats in **Easy Striking** and **Swat the Fly**. Provide a different activity for any child who can swing a pool noodle 'bat' hard enough to hurt another child, if stuck.

Balloons and bubble wrap

Use balloons in activities only if they are covered and you can safely supervise the children using them. Do not use fragile party balloons. Instead use only helium quality balloons or sturdy punch ball balloons. Avoid using latex balloons and any latex product if a child in your care is allergic to latex. Be sure children do not mouth or bite balloons. Make sure every balloon is completely covered. Pantyhose and citrus fruit mesh sacks make effective balloon covers. The covering prevents burst balloons shards from being inhaled by children. An inhaled balloon piece can lodge in a child's throat, causing suffocation. A similar danger is posed by bubble wrap in the activity **Bubble Wrap Jumping**. Be sure children do not put their mouths near or bite the bubble wrap. Be careful to keep the bubble wrap out of the reach of infants, too.

Barriers help keep children safely away from the targets, where objects being thrown could strike them.

Ropes, cords, ribbon, and panty hose

Ropes, cords, ribbon, and pantyhose are used in many of the physical activities in this book. Closely supervise children to be sure that a child does not become entangled in and potentially strangled by one of these items. Balls and balloons are suspended from ropes in the activities **Easy Kicking, Easy Punching**, and **Easy Striking**. If additional protection around the rope is desired, thread the rope through the hollow center of a pool noodle before suspending it, thereby encasing the rope within the pool noodle. Be sure that children do not get the pantyhose entangled around their necks in the activities **Easy Catching, Easy Kicking, Easy Punching**, and **Easy Striking**. Similarly, be sure that the ribbons used to tie small bags around children's waists in **Jump & Shop** do not become entangled around their necks or limbs.

Children pull the loose ends of ropes or pantyhose in the activities **Lug-a-Jug** and **Swat the Fly**. Do not make the ropes longer than necessary and only do these activities if all children can be closely supervised while using the ropes. Store ropes and all equipment where the children are unable to reach them.

Barriers

Barriers help children understand where they are to be during a physical activity. Use a barrier in activities such as **Sock'n Smiley, Newspaper Toss**, and **Sock the Cans**. These barriers help keep children safely away from the targets, where objects being thrown could strike them. Young children sometimes do not understand why barriers are in the way of their fun. They may try to get around the barriers so watch the children closely at all times for safety.

In the activities **Clean Out the Backyard** and **Clean Up the Floor**, barriers are made from ropes tied across the play area. Be sure to drape fabric over the rope and tape it to the rope to make a barrier the children will recognize. Watch the children to be sure no one becomes entangled in the rope.

Figure 10.1 An effective rope and towel barrier for the **Clean Out the Back Yard** kicking and throwing activities.

The
wood blocks
in
Stilt Blocks
are only for
children
to step on
while walking.

Wood blocks

The wood blocks in Stilt Blocks are only for children to step on while walking. Do not do this activity with a child who is likely to swing a wood block by its rope. The child might hit someone with it. Similarly, be sure children do not put the rope loops around their necks because of the possibility of strangulation.

As you lead children in physical activities, try to reinforce...

- Eating healthy food
- Drinking water after doing physical activities
- Academic concepts
- Movement vocabulary
- Spatial relationships
- How our bodies feel when we are physically active

And congratulate the children for...

- Trying new activities
- Learning new fundamental movement skills
- Becoming successful movers
- Having FUN with physical activity

Remember:

• Young children like doing physical activities that are fun and have a purpose they can understand.

• An activity can be designed to allow for children of a variety of ages and abilities to succeed.

• Children need positive feedback and encouraging comments when learning new skills.

• Elimination games keep most children from the practice they need to learn movement skills.

• Young children benefit from structure and routines when learning physical activities.

• Care providers must consider the children's health and safety at all times during physical activities.

The following chapter is the heart of this book. It describes 52 fun physical activities that you can do with young children. Enjoy!

Physical Activities
for Young Children

4

ALL STOP & GO
to MUSIC

View On DVD

All Stop & Go to Music helps children learn to listen. When children hear the music start, they move. When the music stops, they freeze. This is a good activity to do first during physical activity time.

GOALS FOR CHILDREN • Practice running
• Practice listening to cues • Develop cardiovascular endurance

EQUIPMENT
• Music player and lively music
• Safe, large objects to run around, such as pillows and foam pool noodles

INSTRUCTIONS

Children all move in the same direction around a center 'island' of pillows or pool noodles when the music starts. They 'freeze' in place when the music stops. Demonstrate how to move and how to stop. Congratulate children who stop immediately. Ask children to make their feet stay in one place and not move their bodies when the music stops. Suggest that they bend their knees to help themselves stop.

Stopping on cue is important for safety. But it is a difficult skill for young children to learn, and requires lots of practice! Playing **All Stop & Go to Music** many times will teach children to move in the same direction, avoid running into each other, and to stop on cue. The practice is well worth it. Children will become much better at listening and following instructions.

Easier: Teach children the American Sign Language hand signs for 'Stop' and 'Go.' Sign 'Stop' and 'Go' along with the musical cues. Encourage children who might have limited mobility to move in whatever way they can while the music is playing.

Harder: Challenge children to jump, hop, gallop, slide, walk on tiptoes or walk backward when the music begins. School-aged children can take turns helping to lead the activity by starting and stopping the music.

Variety: Ask children to suggest a way that an animal moves and everyone move that way while the music plays.

ALLIGATOR PIT
Suggested by Dana DeCarlo

Crossing an alligator pit on a narrow balance beam is a thrilling challenge for children! The alligator pit is really your floor, the balance beam is a flat foam pool noodle, and the alligator is you!

GOALS FOR CHILDREN • Practice stability

EQUIPMENT

- A 'balance beam' made from two pieces of flat foam pool noodle sections, joined at ends and taped to the floor. Masking tape lines on the carpet will also work.
- Basket
- Many safe objects to carry, such as socks, beanbags, foam puzzle pieces, and pieces of foam cut from pool noodles.
- Duct tape

INSTRUCTIONS

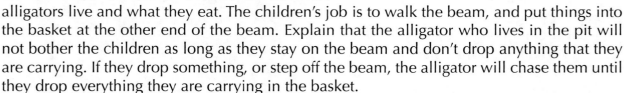

Tape the balance beam to the floor. Place the basket at the far end of the balance beam. Have plenty of small toys and other safe objects for the children to carry at the near end of the beam. Tell the children where alligators live and what they eat. The children's job is to walk the beam, and put things into the basket at the other end of the beam. Explain that the alligator who lives in the pit will not bother the children as long as they stay on the beam and don't drop anything that they are carrying. If they drop something, or step off the beam, the alligator will chase them until they drop everything they are carrying in the basket.

Give each child one item to carry across the beam and drop in the basket. After each child has gone once, increase what each must carry. Vary the skills. Ask children to carry beanbags balanced on their heads and shoulders. Have them jump across with foam blocks between their knees. Let them walk backwards across the beam with arms full of socks. When children drop objects into the pit, or step off the beam, chase them and move your extended arms up and down like an alligator's jaws. School-aged children might enjoy playing the part of the alligator during this activity.

Harder: Give the children more things to carry and harder ways of moving to make this activity more challenging. Tape a curved line on the floor as the balance beam to increase difficulty.

Variety: Pretend that floor spots are 'lily pads.' Arrange spots on the floor and let the children pretend they are frogs that must step, jump or hop from lily pad to lily pad across the alligator pit.

BUBBLE WRAP JUMPING
Inspired by Renée McCall

Tape some bubble wrap to the floor and every child will want to jump until all the bubbles are popped!

GOALS FOR CHILDREN • Practice jumping • Develop cardiovascular endurance

EQUIPMENT

- Bubble wrap, at least a 10 ft. length, 24 inches wide

  Equipment Tip: 1/2 in. bubbles pop best. Ask adults to save wrap for this activity. Some businesses will donate wrap, if asked.

- Clear packaging tape

INSTRUCTIONS

Tape the wrap to the floor so it won't slip. Don't let children mouth or bite the bubble wrap. Instruct the children to move in only one direction when jumping the length of the wrap. No return trips with more than one child jumping at the same time! Or tape a square piece of wrap to the floor for each child if you want them to jump in place.

Show children how to bend their knees and lift with their arms when they jump. Turn on lively music with a strong 4/4 beat to encourage children to jump to the music!

Cues for Learning to Jump for Distance

Just Learning: "Bend your knees." "Start with your arms behind you." "Swing your arms forward as you jump." "Land on both feet at the same time."

More Experienced: "Reach up and out (at a 45° angle) as you jump." "Fall forward when you land." Refer to **On/Off** to learn more jumping cues.

Easier: Hold smaller children's hands for extra balance. Allow children with developmental delays to walk if they are not yet ready to jump.

Harder: Tape 2 ft. squares short distances apart and have school-aged children jump from square to square.

Variety: Have the children walk a 'balance beam' made from a 6 in. wide, 10 ft. long strip of bubble wrap taped to the floor.

CLEAN OUT THE BACKYARD: KICKING

Children will get plenty of practice when you dump a bunch of soft rubber balls and let them clean up the backyard - kicking!

GOALS FOR CHILDREN • Practice kicking • Develop cardiovascular endurance

EQUIPMENT

- Soft rubber balls of different sizes, at least 3 per child
  Indoors use empty plastic gallon milk jugs instead of balls
- A barrier made from a length of rope draped with sheets, lightweight towels, or bright cartoon character fabric
- Sleigh bells or other noisemakers (optional)

INSTRUCTIONS

Divide the play area into half with the rope and fabric barrier. Keep the barrier about three feet off the ground. Hang bells or other noisemakers from the rope for excitement. Dump the same number of balls on each side of the barrier.

Start with an equal number of children on each side of the barrier. Tell the children to kick any balls on their side under the barrier to the other side. The goal is to get all the balls on the other side of the barrier. Hold the hands of younger children to provide the balance they need while learning to kick.

Some children might kick a ball with enough force that it could hurt someone. Give that child a separate and more challenging kicking task. Have him kick the ball as hard as possible across the yard to see how far it goes. Do not allow any child to play **Clean Out the Backyard** in a way that another child could get hurt.

Cues for Learning to Kick

Just Learning: "Stop and step next to the ball." "Look at the ball as you kick it."

More Experienced: "Bring your leg back and then kick." "Kick hard."

Easier: This activity works with most children, regardless of their kicking skills.

Harder: For school-aged children, tie a ribbon around the leg they do not usually kick with. Tell them to kick only with the leg that has the ribbon.

©2008 Diane Craft and Craig Smith

CLEAN OUT THE BACKYARD: THROWING

This activity gives children lots of practice throwing and it's really fun!

GOALS FOR CHILDREN • Practice throwing • Cardiovascular Endurance

EQUIPMENT

- Many soft balls, fuzzy dice, or rolled socks, at least 5 per child
- A barrier made from a length of rope draped with sheets, lightweight towels, or bright cartoon character fabric
- Sleigh bells or other noisemakers (optional)
- Laundry basket to hold balls after activity (optional)

INSTRUCTIONS

Divide the play area into half with the rope and fabric barrier. Keep the barrier about three feet off the ground. Hang bells or other noise-makers from the rope for excitement. Dump the same number of balls on each side of the barrier.

Start with an equal number of children on each side of the barrier. Tell the children to throw any balls on their side over the barrier to the other side. The goal is to get all the balls on the other side of the barrier.

Do not allow children to throw directly at another child's face.

Focus on the Throw, not on Hitting the Target

When helping children learn to throw, focus first on the way in which they are throwing (process) rather than throwing for distance or accuracy (product). In several of the activities in this book, such as **Sock the Cans** and **Sock'n Smiley**, children are throwing at a target. When leading these activities, make the target very large and place it close enough to the children so they can hit it often, even though they are not very accurate at throwing. Use the target only to give some purpose to their throwing, but avoid putting the emphasis on actually hitting the target regularly. Instead, give the children encouragement and feedback on the way in which they are throwing, not on how many targets they can hit. It is difficult to develop a mature throwing technique when preoccupied with hitting the target.

Stages of Throwing

At first, children only move their throwing arm. The rest of the body does not move as they throw. After determining which hand the child usually uses for throwing, ask the child to take a stance with the foot opposite the throwing hand in front of the body. This stance prompts the child to throw using a more advanced technique. As children become better at throwing, they consistently step forward as they throw. But they step forward on the 'wrong' foot. This means that a child who throws with the right arm will step forward with the right foot. Conversely, a child who throws with the left arm will step forward with the left foot. Prompt children to step forward with the foot *opposite* their throwing arm. This is the mature way to throw.

Cues for Learning to Throw

Just Learning: "Look at the target." "Bring the ball to your ear before you throw." "Start with this foot in front" referring to the foot opposite the throwing arm. "Step as you throw." "Point at the target" as you release the ball.

More Experienced: "Stand with your side to the target." "Throw as hard as you can."

Rubber Band Hand and Tape Toe - Suggested by Craig Learn

Place a rubber band on the wrist of the child's throwing arm. Place a piece of tape on the toe of the foot opposite the throwing arm. Prompt the child to throw with the 'rubber band hand' and step with the 'tape toe.'

Easier: Young children can stand next to the barrier and drop objects over. Children with limited mobility can sit next to the barrier and drop the soft objects over.

Harder: Challenge school-aged throwers to see how far back they can stand to throw and still get objects over the barrier.

Variety: Suspend the rope barrier at a height that is over the children's head, drape it with two or more sheets to completely block the view of the other side of the barrier, then have the children throw. It is surprising and funny to see the soft objects come flying 'out of nowhere' from the other side of the barrier. Be sure to stand so that you can see all of the children on both sides of the barrier at all times.

CLEAN UP THE FLOOR

View On
DVD

Indoor throwing practice has never been more fun! Dump a basket full of rolled-up pairs of socks and watch all of the children have a wonderful time cleaning up the floor. This is a great activity for a rainy day.

GOALS FOR CHILDREN • Practice throwing • Develop cardiovascular endurance

EQUIPMENT

- Many pairs of children's socks, at least 5 pairs per child
- A barrier made from a length of rope draped with sheets, light-weight towels, or bright cartoon character fabric
- Sleigh bells or other noisemakers (optional)
- Laundry basket to hold socks after activity (optional)

INSTRUCTIONS

Divide the play area into half by tying the rope between sturdy objects about three feet off the ground. Drape sheets or colorful towels over the rope to make a barrier. Hang bells from the rope to make noise.

Start with an equal number of children on each side of the barrier. Tell the children to throw any socks they find to the other side of the barrier. The goal is to throw all the socks to the other side of the barrier.

Easier: Young children can stand next to the barrier and drop socks over it. Children with limited mobility can sit next to the barrier and drop the soft objects over it.

Harder: Challenge school-aged throwers to see how far back they can stand to throw and still get the socks over the barrier.

Variety: At the end of the activity, bring out the laundry basket. Ask everyone to throw the socks into the basket for clean-up!

COLOR CHALLENGE

This color matching activity provides plenty of physical activity for young children, indoors or out. Children run to put colored foam popsicle sticks or shapes cut from paper on baskets labeled with the same color.

GOALS FOR CHILDREN • Learn color recognition • Develop cardiovascular endurance

EQUIPMENT

- 3 laundry baskets
- Many colored foam popsicle sticks, several of each color - red, yellow, and blue
- 3 large pieces of colored paper, one each of red, yellow and blue
- Circle, square and triangle shapes and alphabet letters cut from colored paper

INSTRUCTIONS

Tape the large sheets of colored papers to the bottom and side of baskets to make one red, one yellow and one blue basket. Place them far away from each other in the play area. Turn the baskets bottom side up to show the colored paper. Give each child a red, yellow or blue color foam popsicle stick. Ask each child to tell you the color of their stick. Tell the children to run to the basket marked with the same color as their sticks, and place their sticks on that basket.

When all sticks are on the baskets, ask each child by name to run to a basket and bring back the color stick you want.

Easier: Very young children or those with developmental delays might enjoy carrying any popsicle stick to any basket.

Harder: Tape letters of the alphabet to the baskets alongside the colored paper. Ask school-aged children to bring cut-out alphabet letters to the correct basket.

Variety: Tape cut-out shapes, such as circles, squares, and triangles to the baskets and have the children bring matching shapes cut from colored paper to the correct baskets.

EASY CATCHING

View On DVD

It takes lots of practice before a young child can catch a tossed ball. Make it easier to learn how to grasp by gently swinging a suspended ball into the child's outstretched arms.

GOALS FOR CHILDREN • Practice catching

EQUIPMENT

- A large, soft ball or a punch ball balloon. Punch ball balloons are much thicker and stronger than party balloons.

- One pair of pantyhose

  Equipment Tip: Stretch the large top part of the pantyhose over a large, soft ball. If using a punch ball balloon, place the deflated balloon inside the open end of the panty-hose, and inflate until it fits snugly. Be sure the balloon is complete-ly covered within the pantyhose. Tie off or cover the end of the pantyhose to prevent balloon pieces from escaping should a balloon burst.

INSTRUCTIONS

Hold the two toes of the pantyhose in one hand, so the ball end of the pantyhose is sus-pended off the floor or ground. Gently swing the ball toward the child's outstretched arms until he grasps it. Repeat this catching activity several times, but stop before he loses inter-est. When he can catch the swung ball easily, try tossing him a soft, fuzzy ball for further catching practice. School-aged children might help by tossing balls to younger children.

Cues for Learning to Catch

Just Learning: "Arms out" prompt children to stand with arms outstretched in front, ready to catch. "Look at the ball."

More Experienced: Aid timing by saying "Ready, catch." Prompt to "Catch with soft hands," or "Give with the ball." "Watch the ball all the way into your hands."

Easier: Lower the ball slowly into the child's outstretched arms until he becomes familiar with grasping the ball.

Harder: For school-aged children, toss a ball that is not held inside pantyhose. Increase the distance the ball is tossed when the child can catch most tosses. Prompt to "Move to the ball."

Variety: Change the size of the ball. Use different balls, such as a beach balls, fabric balls, or playground rubber balls. Suspend the pantyhose from a tree branch or a door frame. Have the child push the ball and catch it as it returns.

EASY KICKING

View On
DVD

Young children need a lot of practice kicking to improve their skill. But kicking a ball means chasing after it to kick it again. A ball suspended in a pair of pantyhose can be kicked repeatedly because it always returns to the kicker!

GOALS FOR CHILDREN • Practice kicking

EQUIPMENT

- Pantyhose, one pair per child
- Lightweight, inflatable balls or large, thick balloons such as 'punch ball balloons,' to go inside the pantyhose
- A support from which to hang the pantyhose and ball. A rope suspended temporarily from wall to wall, five feet high off the floor, will work. A door frame or a tree branch or an overhead cross bar on a piece of playground equipment will also work. Or just hold the toe ends of the pantyhose while the child kicks the ball.

INSTRUCTIONS

Place a deflated ball or 'punch ball' balloon in the open end of a pair of pantyhose. Inflate the ball or balloon until it fits snugly in the pantyhose. Be sure each balloon is completely covered within the pantyhose. Tie off or cover the end of the pantyhose to prevent balloon pieces from escaping if a balloon bursts. Suspend pantyhose from an overhead support so the ball or balloon rests on the floor. Suspend the balls far enough apart so that children will not interfere with each other and the pantyhose will not tangle while kicking. Play some lively music and let the children have fun practicing kicking over and over again. Do not let children wrap pantyhose, or any other rope-like materials around their necks at any time. Use a piece of pool noodle to cover the legs of the pantyhose to prevent wrapping and tangling. Slit the length of the pool noodle along one side and slip it over the pantyhose legs. Refer to **Clean Out the Backyard: Kicking** to learn kicking cues.

Easier: Let children put one hand on a wall, table, or back of a chair to help them balance while kicking. If needed for balance, let children sit as they kick.

Harder: Encourage children to do a running-kick. Have them take a step or two up to the ball before kicking it. For school-aged children, tie a ribbon around the leg they usually do not use when kicking, and have them practice kicking with that leg.

Variety: Place targets in front of the suspended balls. Plastic bowling pins or empty, clean 2-liter plastic bottles filled with colored paper, make great targets.

EASY PUNCHING

Punching balloons helps children develop hand-eye coordination and timing. They need a lot of practice to improve these skills. Maximize punching practice in a small area by suspending punch-ball balloons inside pairs of pantyhose at the children's chest height. Now they can punch and swat these balloons safely many times without having to chase them!

GOALS FOR CHILDREN • Practice punching and striking

EQUIPMENT

- Refer to **Easy Kicking** for equipment required in this activity.

INSTRUCTIONS

Refer to **Easy Kicking** instructions for setting up this activity. Pick a safe area for this punching activity. Suspend pantyhose from an overhead support so the balloons are at the children's chest height. Keep the balloons far enough apart so that children will not interfere with each other and the pantyhose will not tangle while punching. Play some lively music and let the children have fun practicing punching over and over again. Do not let children wrap pantyhose, or any other rope-like materials around their necks at any time. Use a piece of pool noodle to cover the legs of the pantyhose to prevent wrapping and tangling. Slit the length of the pool noodle along one side and slip it over the pantyhose legs.

Easy Punching is an excellent introduction to the fundamental movement skill of striking. After the children can consistently punch or strike the suspended balloon with their open hands, give them short-handled, large-faced lightweight rackets. Make these rackets by inserting a sturdy cardboard tube into a large oven mitt. Duct tape the mitt to the tube. Have the children strike the balloons with the mitt. Also play the activity **Easy Striking**.

Easier: Hold the pantyhose in front of the child's chest, instead of suspending it from above. Children with limited movement, such as due to cerebral palsy, can sit and punch the suspended ball.

Harder: Use less air in the balloons to make the punching target smaller and harder to hit.

Variety: Have two children stand opposite each other and punch the balloon back and forth. Or, have the children catch and toss the balloon back and forth to each other.

EASY STRIKING

 View On DVD

Striking balloons with foam pool noodle bats helps children develop the hand-eye coordination and timing needed in striking games such as badminton, racquetball, tennis and baseball.

GOALS FOR CHILDREN • Practice striking

EQUIPMENT

- Round foam pool noodle bats, one per child
- Also refer to **Easy Kicking** for equipment required in this activity.

INSTRUCTIONS

Refer to **Easy Kicking** instructions for setting up this activity and safety considerations.

Cut one foam pool noodle in half to make two bats. They are ideal for 'batting' practice because they are light in weight, and generally won't hurt if a child is accidentally struck during the activity. Give each child a bat. Play some lively music and let the children have fun striking over and over again. Do not let children wrap pantyhose or any other rope-like materials around their necks at any time. Use a piece of pool noodle to cover the legs of the pantyhose to prevent wrapping and tangling. Slit the length of the pool noodle along one side and slip it over the pantyhose legs.

Helping Children Learn to Strike

To help children grasp the concept of starting the swing with the bat behind them, use the cue "rest the bat on your shoulder before swinging." This is a concrete cue that helps children, who may not yet understand spatial relationship cues, know where to position the bat before swinging. Yet it also can develop bad habits in children who have already mastered the basics of striking. As soon as the children can understand, switch to the cue "hold the bat behind and above your shoulder."

Cues for Learning to Strike

Just Learning: "Look at the ball." "Keep the bat on your shoulder, then swing."

More Experienced: "Stand with your side to the target." "Step forward as you swing."

Easier: At first children are likely to hack or chop at the ball. Use hand-over-hand assistance to help the children learn a level swing. Older, school-aged children could help with this. With practice, and hand-over-hand assistance, children will learn to swing the bat level as they strike the ball.

Let children who have difficulty standing while striking, such as those who use wheelchairs, sit while striking. Lower tethered balls to their seated chest height.

Harder: Use less air in the balloons to make the striking target harder to hit.

Variety: Lower the height of the suspended balloons so they now rest on the floor. Ask the children to pretend that they are playing ice hockey or floor hockey or golf as they strike the balloons on the floor.

45

EGG FARMER

Egg Farmer is a silly activity that delights young children as they chase an egg farmer all over the yard, trying to return the eggs that he dropped.

GOALS FOR CHILDREN • Practice stability • Practice running

EQUIPMENT
- Many plastic eggs, at least 5 per child
- Container to hold eggs
- Funny old hat
- Cloth sack with an egg-sized hole cut in bottom
- Children's plastic outdoor slide – optional

INSTRUCTIONS

Tell the children that an egg farmer will come soon to collect all the eggs chickens have laid. Explain that before the farmer arrives, it's time to pretend to be chickens and lay eggs for the farmer. Have children take plastic eggs, one at a time, and run throughout the yard to 'lay' the eggs anywhere.

After all the eggs are laid, tell the children the egg farmer is on the way. Turn and gaze off in the distance, saying 'I see the egg farmer.' Explain that the egg farmer sometimes has trouble getting all his eggs to market. It will be the children's job to help the farmer find the eggs and keep them all in his sack. Then quickly place an old, funny hat on your head. Turn back to the children and introduce yourself as the egg farmer. Ask the children to run quickly throughout the yard to collect eggs and bring them back.

When all the eggs have been collected, ask the children to help by putting all the eggs into the sack. This is the sack with the hole in the bottom. Hold the hole closed until all the eggs are in. Thank the children for their help, and begin to walk quickly around the yard. As you walk, sing a loud song, and let the eggs start falling out of the hole in the bottom of the sack. Say things out loud like, "I hope I get all my eggs to market today," and "My sack seems lighter. I wonder why?" If children have not yet begun to chase you with the eggs you dropped, look behind and ask the children to bring the dropped eggs to you as you continue to walk briskly around the yard.

Easier: School-aged children can help the younger children find the eggs that the 'chickens' laid. As the egg farmer, drop enough eggs at once so all the children can play. Walk slowly so even the children with little mobility can help the egg farmer get all the eggs back.

Harder: Have the egg farmer walk fast to encourage the children to run to catch up.

Variety: Finish your walk at the base of the children's plastic slide. Let the children take turns rolling eggs down the slide and into the basket.

FEED the PENGUIN

Young children love to run to the other side of the room or yard just to feed 'fish' (stickers) to this hungry penguin.

GOALS FOR CHILDREN • Practice running, jumping, hopping, and galloping

EQUIPMENT

- 1 large picture of a penguin, drawn on poster board with a glossy finish
- Several sheets of colorful stickers

INSTRUCTIONS

Draw a penguin on a large piece of poster board. Stickers come off a glossy surface poster board more easily.

Place the penguin across the room or the yard. Support the penguin against a hard surface to make it easy for children to press against it to put stickers on.

Hint: Remove the paper from around the stickers before giving any stickers to the children. Stickers will come off their paper backing more quickly this way.

Explain that the penguin is hungry. She came all the way from Antarctica to your house to get fed. Her favorite food is fish, so pretend the stickers are fish for the penguin. Give each child a sticker. Have the children run across the room or yard and place their stickers on the penguin. Ask them to return to you for more 'fish' to feed the penguin until she is full.

Play music that goes well with children feeding penguins, such as 'March of the Penguins.'

Remove all of the stickers from the penguin within a few hours of playing so that the clean penguin can be used again for this activity.

Easier: School-aged children can hold the hands of young children who are just learning to walk as they move to feed the penguin. Guide children with visual impairments by placing something that makes noise over the pengun.

Harder: Set up obstacles on the floor or in the yard for children to walk around. Pretend children are climbing over ice flows and swimming underwater beneath the ice as they make their way over and under the obstacles. Vary the way each child has to move to get to the penguin to feed her. Ask school-aged children who already run well to jump or hop on one foot or gallop or slide over to feed the penguin.

Variety: Ask the children to put the stickers on the body parts of the penguin that you name, such as, "Put your stickers on the penguin's belly," or, "Put your stickers on the penguin's beak."

FLOAT THE FISH

Children love Float the Fish. They get to carry water across the yard and pour it into a pipe or a basin and watch plastic fish rise up with the water level! A great activity for a warm summer day in the backyard or park.

GOALS FOR CHILDREN • Practice balance while carrying a liquid

EQUIPMENT

- A large, clean *covered* container for holding several gallons of water, such as a Thermos with a spigot, or easy access to a garden hose or outdoor faucet
- 6 foot length of a large diameter pool noodle with a 2-inch hollow center
  Equipment Tip: With a serrated bread knife, slice a diagonal piece from one end of the pool noodle to form a trough to catch water (see photo above)
- A plastic basin 4 inches deep
- One or two small rubber or plastic fish that will float in water
- Water containers such as clean paper cups or small watering cans or recycled 1 liter water bottle (discard screw-on tops), one per child
- Duct tape

INSTRUCTIONS

Duct tape the cut end of the pool noodle to a fence or upside-down laundry basket, keeping it 2 feet higher than the uncut end. Tape the uncut lower end of the pool noodle to the basin on the ground, so that water poured through the pool noodle drains into the basin.

Place the plastic fish in the dry basin.

Fill the large container with about 2 gallons of clean tap water. Always keep this container covered, to prevent children from losing their balance and falling into the container. A garden hose or outdoor faucet can also be used to fill children's water containers.

Place the source of water at least 40 feet from the pool noodle set-up so children will get lots of physical activity moving between where they get the water and where they pour the water.

The excitement of this activity, and the motivation for children to be physically active, come from the children realizing they can help the fish. Yes, the children know the fish are plastic, but when it's explained that fish need water to breathe, just as we need air to breathe, they focus on how they can help the fish by bringing them water.

Explain to the children that there are fish in the dry basin. The children have to bring water to help the fish float and breathe. Stress that the children have to *help* the fish!

Give each child a water container, and demonstrate the safe way to fill the container with water. Explain that the water is for the fish only. If anyone is thirsty, have them drink from the usual source before the activity. The first thing two-year-olds want to do during this activity is drink the water they are carrying!

School-aged children can help the younger children fill their water containers. Each child begins the activity as soon as there is water to carry. Some children become so excited during this activity that they spill all their water before they get to the fish! Covered sipper cups or plastic 1-liter bottles will help them arrive with water.

Easier: Although the pool noodle 'straw' makes this activity more interesting, just having the children carry the water directly to the basin to float the fish makes the activity set-up easier, and pouring the water is not as difficult.

This can be a great activity for a child with cerebral palsy, or other special needs, who uses a wheelchair and may have dificulty with motor control. Position the child next to the pool noodle 'straw' and guide her in lifting the water container into position and in pouring water down the 'straw.'

FROG CATCHER

Hungry little frogs move around the room or yard looking for tasty bugs. But they have to be careful because there's a frog catcher at the pond!

GOALS FOR CHILDREN • Practice leaping like a frog • Practice stability • Develop cardiovascular endurance • Develop upper body strength and endurance

EQUIPMENT

- Floor spots to be used as lily pads
- A net, made from open mesh fabric, approximately 5 foot by 5 foot
- Pictures or drawings of insects printed on card stock, at least 5 picture cards per child

  Equipment tip: Pictures of insects are available from the Internet.

INSTRUCTIONS

Talk about frogs living in ponds and eating insects. Explain that they sit safely on lily pads in the sun when not chasing insects. Tell the children that sometimes people catch frogs with nets, when frogs are not on their lily pads.

Ask the children to pretend to be frogs. Place many picture cards of tasty insects around the room or yard. The children will frog-leap from their lily pads (floor spots) to catch the insects, and frog-leap back to the safety of their lily pads with the insects.

Demonstrate how to leap like a frog. Frogs start squatting with all limbs on the floor. When they leap like a frog, they move both hands forward, keeping their body weight on the feet. Then they jump both feet forward, while shifting their body weight toward the hands. Have the children practice leaping like a frog.

Spread the insect picture cards within jumping distance of the children's lily pads. Have the children jump to get the insects. Warn the children to quickly jump back to the safety of their lily pads when the frog catcher comes to the pond!

While they are busy leaping like frogs, pretend to try and catch them in your mesh net. Throw the net partially over them and then complain when they get away from you!

Easier: Allow younger children to walk or run, instead of leaping like frogs, as they collect insects.

Harder: Place the insects farther away from the lily pads for school-aged children.

Variety: Tell the children there's a hungry frog that is unable to jump, who lives on the other side of the pond. Ask them to bring some of the insects that they catch to the other side of the pond to help feed the hungry frog.

Include a child who uses a wheelchair by giving him a pool noodle. His job is to 'catch' children by tapping them as they go by, leaping like frogs.

GARDEN FRIENDS

Children have fun creating a pretend garden, running across the room or yard to place animal cut-outs next to, above, and below flowers.

GOALS FOR CHILDREN • Learn spatial relationships of 'next to,' 'above,' and 'below'
• Practice running, jumping, hopping and galloping

EQUIPMENT

- 6 large flowers made from different color construction paper
- Smaller construction paper birds, rabbits and butterflies, at least five cutouts per child
- Masking tape

INSTRUCTIONS

Make brightly colored construction paper cutouts of birds, rabbits, and butterflies. Also cut-out large flowers, each from a different color. Laminating the flowers and other cut-outs will help them last. Place rounds of masking tape on the back of all of the cut-outs. Tape the six large flowers to a wall or door, at the far end of the room. Outdoors, tape the large flowers to the side of a playhouse, or some other sturdy vertical surface, across the yard. Spread the animal cut-outs, tape side up, on a table or the floor next to the children.

Tell the children that they are going to bring some animal friends to a garden. They will take one cut-out from the pile next to them, run across the room or yard to the 'garden,' and stick the cut-out in the *exact* spot you tell them. Demonstrate and explain, "I get one animal cut-out from the pile and run to the garden. Then I place it *'next to'* the large blue flower. Now I run back to the pile of cut-outs and get another. This one I carry to the garden and place it *'above'* the green flower. I run back to the pile for another cut-out, run to the garden, and place it *'below'* to the large white flower."

Begin the activity. Focus on helping children find the correct position, while they learn the meaning of the spatial relationship terms 'next to,' 'above,' and 'below.' School-aged children can enjoy this activity or help the younger children position their cut-outs.

Easier: Young children might not be ready to understand spatial relationship terms. Ask them to put the cut-outs anywhere near the large flowers in the 'garden.'

Harder: Vary locomotor skills. Ask children to jump, hop, gallop, or slide. Ask school-aged children to place cut-outs 'beside,' to the 'right side,' to the 'left side,' or 'adjacent to' the flowers.

Variety: Change the theme of this activity to placing paper cut-out cars in a street, or airplanes at the airport. Always emphasize the spatial relationship among objects. Make some of the cut-outs from sandpaper and felt. These will help children pay attention to differences in textures.

GO FISHING

Go Fishing has children run or jump or hop across the room or yard repeatedly, looking for matches to the Go Fish cards they are carrying.

GOALS FOR CHILDREN • Practice running, jumping, hopping and rolling
• Learn object, shape and color recognition

EQUIPMENT

• One deck of *Go Fish cards*

INSTRUCTIONS

Sort the deck of cards into two identical piles. For example, place three shark cards in one pile and three matching shark cards in the other pile. Place the cards from one pile face up in the 'sea' at the far end of the room or yard. Place the cards from the other pile at the near end of the room or yard next to the children and you.

Ask each child to choose one Go Fish card. Have them run or jump or hop across the room or yard to the 'sea' where the other Go Fish cards are piled. Ask them to find the match to their card. Have them return and show you the match. Give them new cards, and do the activity until all of the cards are matched. School-aged children can help by bringing cards back to the 'sea' pile so the activity can continue.   As time permits, ask children questions about the creatures on the cards, such as, "What is the creature called? What color is it? Does it ever leave the sea and go on land?"

Refer to **Running with Streamers** to learn running cues.

Easier: School-aged children can help younger children match their cards.

Harder: Ask older children to gallop or skip or even roll, if the surface permits, to and from the sea creature pile.

Variety: Use this and other activities in this book to encourage speech among children with speech delays. Often they display their best expressive speech when they are involved in active play. Encourage speech by talking with and asking children questions about the game they are playing.

HEALTHY
FOOD HUNTING

View On DVD

Healthy Food Hunting helps children learn the names of fruits and vegetables that are healthy and nutritious. They get a good workout, too, practicing loco-motor skills as they move around matching picture cards.

GOALS FOR CHILDREN • Practice jumping, hopping, sliding, galloping, and tiptoeing • Practice matching objects •Practice identifying healthy foods

EQUIPMENT

• Several sets of homemade picture cards of fruits and vegetables. See instructions on next page.

INSTRUCTIONS

Spend two minutes showing children the fruit and vegetable cards. Discuss the name of each fruit and vegetable, and where each grows. Has anyone tasted each food? Talk about how eating fruits and vegetables is healthy for us. They contain vitamins and minerals that our bodies need to grow and stay healthy, they taste good, and they make great snacks.

Explain that each child will get a card showing a fruit or a vegetable. Place all the mates to the cards at the opposite side of the room or yard. Ask the children to do one of the fol-lowing: jump, hop, gallop, slide, or tip-toe across the room or yard to the pile of cards, find the card that looks exactly like the one they have been carrying, and bring the pair back to you. As soon as a child returns with a match, give him another card to match, so there is no waiting. Ask him to name the fruit or vegetable on the card before he moves to find its mate.

Share a snack made from one or more of the same real fruits and vegetables after playing!

Easier: Help children find the matching cards. Ask children to simply walk or run.

Harder: Ask older children to move greater distances to find their card's mate. Ask them to practice more difficult locomotor skills, such as slide, hop and skip. School-aged children can help you keep the activity going by returning cards to the opposite side of the room or yard, as you keep handing out cards for the younger children to match.

Variety: Hide the mates to cards under objects throughout the room or yard.

Making food cards for **Healthy Food Hunting**, **Jump & Shop**, **Stocking Grocery Shelves**, and **Paper Plate Scooters**:

Clip art pictures of fruits and vegetables are available on the Internet. Find them and print them in color, if possible. Trim and glue them to a 4 x 6 index card. Add the names of the fruits and vegetables to each card. Most young children will not be ready to read, but provide the names for those who are curious about words. Some children with autism might already be able to read these words. Cut the pictures to 4 inch x 6 inch card size. Laminate the food cards for durability.

Fruit Suggestions
Apple, Banana, Grapefruit, Grape, Lemon, Lime, Mango, Orange, Papaya, Peach, Pear, Strawberry

Vegetable Suggestions
Asparagus, Carrot, Celery, Corn, Cucumber, Green Pepper, Lettuce, Okra, Onion, Pea, Potato, Tomato

Laminated cards shown here are each 4.5 x 3.5 inches.

HOOP BUS

Young children love to pretend to 'drive' a hula hoop car with an adult or older child as a passenger inside.

GOALS FOR CHILDREN • Practice stability

EQUIPMENT

• Hula hoops, one per two players

INSTRUCTIONS

An adult or school-aged child and one young child squeeze into a hula hoop together, holding the hoop near the taller person's waist level. The older person moves slowly around the floor, steering the younger child. After a short time, have the younger child take the 'wheel' and steer around the room or yard! Some children might not want to share the inside of the hoop with anyone. Let them drive 'solo' or guide their hoop from behind. Too much force on the hoop can bend it out of shape. Bent hoops will not roll well. So save them for use in activities such as this and **Hoop Scotch**.

Easier: The larger person stands outside the hoop, guiding it from behind. If guiding a child with visual impairment, guide from the front.

Harder: Resist the child's pull a bit to give the child a better workout.

Variety: Pretend each hula hoop is a postal truck, and deliver 'mail' to different places in the house or yard.

HOOP CHASE

Roll hoops across the yard or park. Children run after the hoops and try to catch them before the hoops slow down and settle to the ground.

GOALS FOR CHILDREN • Practice running • Practice catching

EQUIPMENT

• Hula hoops, one per child

INSTRUCTIONS

Stand in the center of the yard or park. Roll a hula hoop away from the center with a bowling motion. Call a child's name as you roll the hoop. The child named is to chase the hoop, catch it before it stops rolling, and return the hoop to the center of the yard. Pretend each hoop is trying to escape from the 'hoop-pen', and the children are 'hoop-wranglers' who have to catch and return the hoops to the pen.

Demonstrate how the activity is done before having the children do it. Be sure the play area is safe and free of obstructions.

Easier: Roll hoops a short distance for younger children. Roll the hoop directly to a child who uses a wheelchair, so the challenge is to catch the hoop without chasing it.

Harder: Roll hoops farther for older children.

Variety: Roll two hoops and let the child decide which one to catch. Enlist older, school-aged children to roll the hoops.

HOOP LIMBO

How low can they go! Angle a hoop as children try to go through it and see the creative ways they invent to get through!

GOALS FOR CHILDREN • Practice stability

EQUIPMENT

- Hula hoops
- Limbo music

INSTRUCTIONS

Hold a hula hoop straight up-and-down, with the rim touching the floor. Or support the hoop on either side by taping it between two laundry baskets. Ask the children to 'limbo' through the hoop, one at a time, to lively limbo music. Change the angle of the hoop to 'lower the bar' after each successful round.

Demonstrate how the activity is done before having the children do it.

Enlist the help of school-aged children in holding the hoops, as well as giving them the chance to limbo themselves. This activity provides needed practice for children who have difficulty with body awareness.

Easier: It's okay if children choose not to 'limbo' though the hoop, substituting their own way to go through that's more comfortable for them.

Harder: Hold the hoop at a sharp angle to make the opening smaller. Use two hoops together, one inside the other, and change the opening size by twisting the hoops (see photo above).

Variety: Make an obstacle course of several hoops at different angles for the children to limbo through.

HOOP RIGHT THROUGH

This is a great activity to teach children the names of the parts of their bodies, and to give them practice with understanding the meaning of the word *through*.

GOALS FOR CHILDREN • Practice stability
• Learn spatial relationships • Learn body parts

EQUIPMENT

• Hula hoops, one per child

INSTRUCTIONS

Hold a hula hoop straight up-and-down, with the rim touching the floor. Demonstrate what putting a leg 'through' the hoop looks like. Then they ask the children, "Can you put your leg through your hoop?" After the children have shown they can put their legs through the hoop successfully, then ask "Can you put your arm through the hoop?" Then ask the same for foot, head and hand. Prompt children with language delays to say or sign the name of each body part as you play.

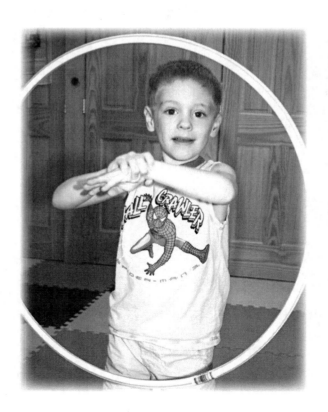

When the children understand these body parts well, introduce the body parts of elbows, shoulders and ankles. As the final task, ask the children "Can you put YOU through the hoop?" Assist children as needed. School-age children can be very helpful assisting with this activity by holding the hoop, giving instructions and demonstrating the parts of the body.

HOOP SCATTERBALL

Children get lots of practice running when they chase balls and plastic bottles that try to get away from them.

GOALS FOR CHILDREN • Practice running

EQUIPMENT

- Hula hoops
- 6 playground balls or 6 empty, clean 2-liter plastic bottles

INSTRUCTIONS

Lay two hoops on the floor in the center of the room. Put several playground balls or empty 2-liter bottles in the center of the hoops. Explain to the children that the balls (or bottles) live in the hoops, and have to stay there. Ask the children to help you return any that try to escape. Then gently kick a few balls or bottles from the hoop and shout, "They're getting away! Bring them back to the hoops!" Have the children run after all the balls or bottles you kick. Control the pace of the activity to allow all the children to run and retrieve some balls or bottles.

The children may modify this game so they are the ones kicking the balls and bottles. This is okay, as long as their play is safe. Just reverse roles and bring the balls or bottles back to the hoops so the children stay active.

Easier: Kick the balls or bottles gently so they don't travel far from the hoops.

Harder: Kick the balls or bottles hard and in different directions.

Variety: Reverse roles and have the children kick the balls or bottles from the hoops.

HOOP SCOTCH

Hoop Scotch is for young children just learning how to play Hop Scotch. Hoops take the place of numbered squares, and children get to throw their beanbags into any hoop they want.

GOALS FOR CHILDREN • Practice jumping or hopping • Practice throwing • Practice stability

EQUIPMENT

- Hula hoops, one per child
- Beanbags, one per child
  Equipment Tip: Make beanbags from children's old socks. Partially fill socks with rice or small beans. Sew the ends of socks shut to keep beans from spilling, and the children from putting the beans in their mouths.

INSTRUCTIONS

Hoop Scotch is like Hop Scotch, but uses hoops lying on the floor in any pattern you choose. Ask children to toss their beanbags into the hoops, jump or hop into the hoop to get the beanbags, and jump or hop out of the hoop with the beanbags. Let the children choose into which hoops to toss. Demonstrate how to do the activity then have the children try it.

Cues for Learning to Hop

"Hop on just one foot." "Keep your other foot off the ground." "Lift a little with your arms as you hop."

Easier: Let children stand close to a hoop and step, rather than jump or hop, into the hoop.

Harder: Ask school-aged children to stand farther from the hoops. Place the hoops in a line. Have them throw into and retrieve from each hoop in sequence.

HOOP TARGET

Children love to throw socks at the noisy target made by hanging aluminum pie plates from a hula hoop!

GOALS FOR CHILDREN • Practice throwing

EQUIPMENT

- Hula hoops, one per child
- One laundry basket
- Aluminum pie plates
- String
- Duct tape
- Rolled socks, at least 5 per child

INSTRUCTIONS

Jam a hoop upright inside a laundry basket (see photo at right.) Fasten the hoop to the sides of the basket with duct tape. Hang inviting targets, such as a few aluminum pie plates, by string from the top of the hoop. Indoors, hang a hula hoop from the top of a door frame. Place a basket below. Ask the children to throw rolled socks at the target.

Children love the noise the pie plates make when hit by the socks!

Refer to **Clean Out the Backyard** to learn throwing cues.

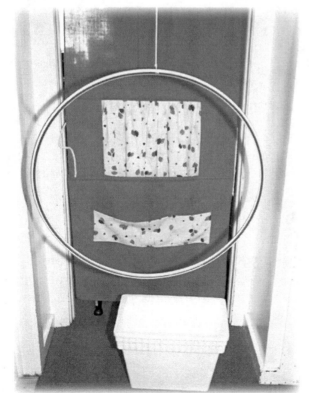

Easier: Have children stand closer to the target while throwing.

Harder: Have children stand farther away from the target while throwing.

JUMP & SHOP

View On DVD

In **Jump & Shop** children get plenty of physical activity pretending to jump around like kangaroos shopping for nutritious foods.

GOALS FOR CHILDREN • Practice identifying nutritious foods
• Practice stability • Practice jumping

EQUIPMENT

- One small paper 'gift' bag per child
- Length of thin, gift-wrap ribbon to thread through small slits on the bag
- Several sets of fruit and vegetable food cards. See how to make food cards in the activity **Healthy Food Hunting.**

INSTRUCTIONS

Make 'pouches' from small, sturdy, gift bags. Thread ribbons through small slits in the bags to make 'belts.' Tie the bags around the children's waists. Keep the bags in front, like kangaroos' pouches.

Spend a few minutes showing children the fruit and vegetable cards, one at a time. Talk about the importance of eating healthy food.

Play lively music as children jump around 'shopping' for healthy food cards and put them in their pouches. Follow the activity with a snack featuring one of the healthy fruits or vegetables from the activity.

He knows this is not the healthiest choice!

Refer to **Bubble Wrap Jumping** and **On/Off** to learn jumping cues.

Easier: Children who tire after several jumps might walk and pick up food cards for the rest of the activity. Hold the hand of a highly distractable child and guide him or her to find, gather and hand the food card to you.

Harder: Jumping continuously during this activity is very demanding. There is no need to make this activity harder.

Variety: Distribute food cards of both nutritious and not so nutritious foods. Ask the children to jump and shop only for foods that keep us healthy. School-aged children can play a variation of **Hoop Scotch** in which children toss and retrieve food cards instead of beanbags.

LAND/LAKE

View On
DVD

Taught to us by Julie Lopez

Land/Lake helps children develop listening skills while enjoying physical activity. Children jump to a green floor spots when the adult says 'Land.' They jump to blue floor spots when the adult says 'Lake.' Play the activity **On/Off** first several times, until children get used to following directions. Then challenge them with **Land/Lake**. After playing these activities, children become much better at listening and following instructions. These are important skills for success in school.

GOALS FOR CHILDREN • Practice jumping • Develop listening skills

EQUIPMENT

• Green (land) and blue (lake) floor spots, one of each color per child. If blue and green floor spots are not available, put colored tape lines of two different colors on the floor. Children then jump from one line to the other.

INSTRUCTIONS

Start with all children standing on their blue (lake) floor spots, opposite their green (land) spots, a short jump away.

Shout either "Land!" or "Lake!" The children must quickly jump to their green spots if you shouted, "Land!" or remain on their blue spots if you shouted "Lake." Tease the children by dragging out the 'La' sound before saying 'Land' or 'Lake.'

When children make mistakes, playfully redirect them to the correct position with words of encouragement. This is not an elimination game. Congratulate children when they follow instructions.

Refer to **Bubble Wrap Jumping** and **On/Off** to learn jumping cues.

Easier: Place the floor spots closer for less skilled jumpers. Let the youngest children just jump where they are standing until they are old enough to understand the game. For children with very limited movement, put the floor spots on their wheelchair trays. Ask them to touch, instead of jump to, the spot that is called.

Harder: Some children can jump farther than others. Angle the floor spots or tape lines so skilled children have to jump farther than less skilled children.

Variety: School-aged children can enjoy taking the adult's role of calling 'Land' or Lake.'

©2008 Diane Craft and Craig Smith

LAUNDRY PICK-UP

 View On DVD

Pretend to carelessly drop laundry all over the floor or yard. Young children will happily run and pick it all up and bring it back to you!

GOALS FOR CHILDREN • Practice running, jumping, galloping

EQUIPMENT

- One laundry basket
- Many pairs of socks, at least five pairs of socks for each child

INSTRUCTIONS

Tell the children that you have some laundry in the basket that you have to put away. Explain that sometimes you are messy. Laundry might fall out of the basket, onto the floor or ground, before you get to put it away. Ask them to help you if any falls out.

Walk around the room or yard quickly, throwing socks wildly from the basket in every direction. Say out loud, "I'm so messy, I'm so messy. I'll never get this laundry put away unless some children help me bring the laundry back!"

Continue walking briskly around the yard throwing socks. After the basket is empty, place it on the floor or ground. Encourage children to help you by picking up the socks and returning them to the basket.

School-aged children might enjoy the job of being the 'messy' laundry thrower.

Refer to **Puzzle Carry** to learn galloping cues.

Easier: Drop socks near younger children or children with limited mobility to make it easier for them to participate.

Harder: Walk across the yard a good distance before dropping the socks, and return to the other side where you set the basket. Now children have to run further to bring the socks back to put them in the basket. Challenge older children to jump or gallop during the activity.

Variety: Place the empty basket at the foot of a toy slide and have the children roll the balled socks down the slide into the basket after they have retrieved them.

This is a great activity for a child with limited grasping ability, perhaps due to cerebral palsy. Drop a sock on the child's head or directly in front of the child. Encourage him or her to pick it up and place it in the nearby basket.

LETTER TO A FRIEND

In **Letter to a Friend,** children learn how to create and mail a letter. They run, jump, tiptoe, and walk backward, crossing the play area to put children's picture cards into the envelope, and stick on pretend stamps.

GOALS FOR CHILDREN • Practice running, jumping, tiptoeing and walking backward

EQUIPMENT

- One large brown envelope
- One deck of children's playing cards, such as Go Fish
- One sheet of large stickers
- Tape
- Marker

INSTRUCTIONS

Ask the children to name a child who used to be in your program. Tell children they are going to pretend to send that child some mail.

Write the name of the child and a mailing address on the envelope, explaining each of the parts of a mailing address.

Tape the open envelope, opening side up, to a firm surface across the yard or room.

Give each child a card from the deck. Tell the children to run across the yard or room and put the card in the envelope. Continue until all the cards are in the envelope. Vary the way the children have to move across the area.

Next, give the children large stickers, pretnding they are stamps. Ask them to run across the area and put the stickers on the outside of the envelope.

Easier: Hold unsteady walkers' hands as they move to and from the envelope.

Harder: Vary the way children are to move to and from the envelope. Ask school-aged children to hop, gallop, slide, skip and leap. These are more difficult locomotor skills than running.

Variety: Give the children each one envelope. Set up different stations in the play area. Have them move from station to station, getting papers to put in the envelope at one station, stickers at another, and markers at a third. Have the final station be the pretend mailbox. Let them mail as many letters as they want, moving quickly between stations as they prepare their letters.

Many children with visual impairments habitually move slowly. Guide children who are blind to and from the envelope, encouraging fast walking, or even running.

LUG-A-JUG

View On DVD

Lug-a-Jug is a fun outdoor activity for children. It helps them develop upper body strength and it lets them show everyone how strong they are at the same time! Plastic milk containers filled with water are heavy to lift. They slide along the ground well, though, when pulled by ropes or pairs of panty hose threaded though their handles.

GOALS FOR CHILDREN • Practice stability
• Develop upper body strength and endurance

EQUIPMENT

- Many different sizes of used plastic milk jugs, such as quart, half-gallon and gallon, with handles and caps

- Duct tape for securing caps to containers after they are filled with water

- Rope or pantyhose to slip through the handles of the jugs for pulling

INSTRUCTIONS

Wash and clean many different sizes of used plastic milk or water jugs. Fill each with water and secure caps to jugs with Duct tape. Slip lengths of rope or pantyhose through jug handles. Demonstrate how the jugs can be pulled along the ground as you show the children where they can go while hauling. Give each child a jug to drag and prepare to be amazed at how hard the children work dragging the jugs!

Easier: Give smaller children lighter, smaller or partially filled jugs to drag.

Harder: Give school-aged children two or more jugs to pull at one time.

Variety: Some children might enjoy just picking up the jugs and carrying them a short distance. Show them the proper way to lift a heavy object by bending their knees while keeping their backs straight.

A child who uses a wheelchair can play by lifting the jug into her lap and wheeling it to her destination.

MATCHING NUMBERS

View On DVD

Inspired by Doreen Aristy

In **Matching Numbers**, children run across the room or yard, carrying a numbered card. They must find the pocket labeled with the same number, put the card in that pocket, and return to take another card.

GOALS FOR CHILDREN • Practice running, jumping, galloping, hopping, and sliding
• Learn numbers and number sequencing

EQUIPMENT

• Two decks of homemade or purchased number cards. Each deck has four sets of cards numbered from one to twelve. Use index cards if making them yourself.
• Three manila folders, each having four pockets attached

INSTRUCTIONS

Prepare the manila folders and cards in advance. Instructions are on the next page.

Tape the folders next to each other on a wall or other flat surface. Show the children the card decks and the folders. Demonstrate how the cards match the pockets, and how the cards fit into the pockets. Ask the children to identify the numbers as you hold up each card.

Scatter the cards on the floor at the opposite side of the room or yard. Have the children take one card each, and run, jump, tiptoe, hop, or gallop to the correct folder and put their cards in the proper pocket. Children then return to get another card.

After all the cards are in the folder pockets, remove the cards from each pocket. Count aloud to twelve with the children as you point to each number, in turn, on the folders.

Easier: Lead younger children to the correct pocket, or allow them to put their cards in any pocket. Lower the height of folders to make pockets easy to reach for smaller children.

Harder: Ask school-aged children to select cards with numbers that when added equal the number on the slot into which the two cards will be placed. An example would be a child places the cards numbered 1 and 3 in the slot labeled 4, because 1 + 3 equal 4.

Variety: Instead of numbers, have the children match shapes and colors. Create separate decks of cards showing animals and their homes, and the names of animals with pictures of animals.

Making number cards and folders for the activity **Matching Numbers**:

To make number cards, write the numbers one through twelve, one number per card, on the front of the card. On the reverse of each card, spell the word for that number. Then draw and color a corresponding number of a single shape, such as diamonds, circles, squares, or triangles, on the number side of the card.

The folders are made from plain manila folders from the dollar store. Buy twice as many as you need to make the folders for the activity, because the pockets are cut from one manila folder and glued to another. Cut the pockets wider than the cards. Leave a margin of folder material around the pockets for gluing onto the other folder. Be sure to make the pocket pieces wide and deep enough to easily hold four cards at once. Test to be sure children can insert cards into and remove cards from the pockets without difficulty. Fold the margins around the pockets so they are under the pockets. Glue the margins of the pockets to the surface of the uncut manila folder.

Take one set of cards and glue them to the front of the twelve pockets on the folders. Glue cards 1-4 on the pockets of the first folder, 5-8 on the second, and 9-12 on the third. Two pockets go on the top half of the folder, and two on the bottom half, as shown below. Have the card side with the number and the shapes showing.

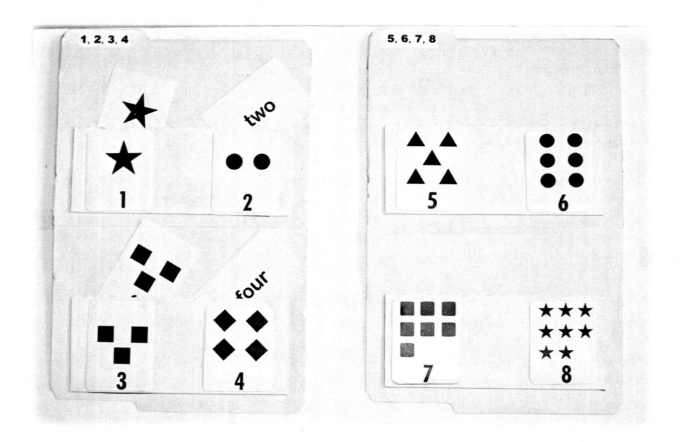

MATCHING SOCKS

(View On DVD)

Matching Socks gets children of all ages running through the room or yard to find the sock that matches the one they are carrying.

GOALS FOR CHILDREN • Practice running, jumping, galloping, hopping, and sliding
• Practice object recognition

EQUIPMENT

• Five pairs of socks per child. Have different colors, patterns and sizes of socks available.

INSTRUCTIONS

Separate pairs of socks into two identical piles. Scatter the socks from one pile throughout the room or yard. Spend a few minutes explaining differences in socks. Talk about colors, patterns, and sizes. Ask if a large and a small sock or a blue and a brown sock match? Will a striped sock match a plain black sock? Help the children understand what is meant by a match.

Give each child a sock from the pile. Ask the children to run and find the matching sock, and bring the pair back to you. Then give each child a new sock to match until they are all matched.

School-aged children can help by placing socks throughout the room or yard.

Easier: Lead younger children to the correct sock match, and discuss with them why the socks match.

Harder: Show school-aged children the sock they must match, but do not let them take the sock with them when looking for the match.

Variety: Have the children match colors, such as any blue sock, or size, such as any adult-sized sock, or patterns, such as any striped sock.

MUSICAL HOOPS

This is a cooperative version of the game Musical Chairs. Children are not eliminated during the game. Instead, hoops are taken away each round. The children have fun sharing the remaining hoops.

GOALS FOR CHILDREN • Practice running

EQUIPMENT

- Hula hoops, one per child
- Music player

INSTRUCTIONS

Place hula hoops on the floor throughout the area, leaving plenty of room around the edge of the area for the children to run.

Explain that when the music starts, the children are to run around the outside of the room, with everyone running in the same direction. When the music stops, each child must find a hoop and stand inside it. Tell them that the next time the music stops, they must share a hoop with another child if they cannot find an empty hoop. Demonstrate the activity.

Ask each child to stand in a hoop. Start the music. After a few loops around the hoops, stop the music. When all the children are in hoops, dramatically remove one hoop from the game, leaving fewer hoops than children.

Repeatedly start and stop the music, removing another hoop each time. The activity ends when all of the children are sharing the one remaining hoop. They may need to help each other in order for everyone to get at least one foot inside the remaining hoop. Encourage the children to congratulate each other on sharing.

Easier: Very young, or highly distractible children may need you to hold their hands as they walk, rather then run, around the outside of the hoops. They may also need help finding an available hoop.

Harder: Vary the locomotor skill children use each time you restart the music. Ask school-aged children to jump, or hop, or tiptoe, or walk backward.

NEWSPAPER TOSS

Inspired by Mary Anne Torbert

View On DVD

This activity gives children of all ages many chances to practice throwing. They love the noise the pie plates make when hit. It is also a good activity for adults to instruct children how to throw properly.

GOALS FOR CHILDREN • Practice throwing

EQUIPMENT

- Rolled newspapers, about 12 per child
- Masking tape
- 1 laundry basket
- 1 hula hoop
- 3 aluminum pie plates
- String
- Duct tape
- Barrier

INSTRUCTIONS

Make this noisy target by wedging a hula hoop into the basket so it remains vertical. Duct tape the hoop securely to the side of the basket. Suspend three pie plates with string from the top of the hoop.

Tightly roll two folded sheets of newsprint into a 'log.' Use masking tape to keep the paper rolled. Place the assembled basket-target behind a low barrier large enough to keep children on the front side, away from the target.

Demonstrate throwing toward the target from behind the barrier. Dump the newspapers in front of the barrier and let the children throw them toward the target.
Watch the children throw. Do they bring the newspaper to a position next to their ears before throwing? Do they step forward with the feet opposite their throwing arms as they throw? Do they follow through by bringing their arms down diagonally across their bodies? Prompt them to throw in a more mature manner. Physically assist children who need help learning to throw properly.

When the newspapers have all been thrown, bring the full basket from behind the barrier and dump the newspapers in front. Put the basket-target back in position and let the children resume throwing.

Refer to **Clean Out the Backyard: Throwing** to learn throwing cues.

Easier/Harder: Angle the barrier so children on one end are much closer to the target than children at the other end. Encourage the more mature school-aged throwers to stand farther away from the target when they throw. Less skilled children stand closer to the target. Children need to succeed to enjoy a task!

Variety: Toss soft plush toys, rolled socks or foam balls at the target when enjoying this activity indoors in a small area.

OBSTACLE COURSE: INDOOR Inspired by Pat Hubbard

An indoor obstacle course can give children fundamental movement skill practice. Creating a safe one takes some planning. Once in place, though, it can engage children in many physical, academic and art activities.

Children like obstacle courses because they challenge both mind and body. They help children develop coordination and muscular strength and endurance. Children also learn about spatial relationships when told to climb over, crawl through and duck under objects.

Safe obstacle courses can be made from items available in most homes. Sofa cushions and pillows covered with sheets become mountains and valleys. Floor spots become stones to jump on when crossing an alligator-infested carpet. Crepe streamers taped to the ceiling in the corner of a room become a jungle, or a tropical rain forest. A sleeping bag or blanket thrown over chairs makes a tunnel.

Indoor obstacle courses can stretch from room to room. It might not be possible to loop back to join the last obstacle with the first. If so, think of a theme for the course to guide the children from start to finish. Give their journey a purpose. For example, make children 'Jungle Explorers' looking for rare stuffed toys. They

Two children explore a streamer forrest

can be 'Snack Hunters' travelling the world to find delicious, nutritious snacks at the end of the course. Have the children cross a pretend swamp. Make them go through a crepe paper streamer jungle. Let them crawl though a maze or tunnel. Watch them climb over seat cushion mountains on their journey. Along the way have them jump from lily pad to lily pad to avoid the alligators on the carpet. Play musical instruments to warn away any jungle animals. Make traveling the course seem like a real adventure. After a few times through the course, conduct other activities using the course. Read stories in the jungle. Listen to music sitting on the mountains. Do art projects and carry them through the tunnel. Be creative!

GOALS FOR CHILDREN • Practice stability
• Practice jumping and climbing • Learn spatial relationships
• Practice sequencing tasks • Develop muscular strength and endurance

EQUIPMENT

- Sofa and chair cushions
- Pillows
- Laundry baskets
- Chairs
- Carpet squares
- Bubble wrap paths, taped in place
- Hula hoops
- Blankets, sheets or sleeping blanket
- Toy animals
- Crepe paper streamers, tape
- Cloth-draped table
- Bubble wrap paths, taped in place

Jumping on lily pads

INSTRUCTIONS

Choose only objects that you know to be safe and in good condition for the course. If you move a piece of furniture, be sure it is stable and safe in its new position.

Choose obstacles that children can climb over, go under, and crawl through. Design the course so children have to jump or hop from place to place. Make them move around objects. Let them punch or kick balloons suspended in pantyhose before climbing the next obstacle. Add sequencing tasks to the course. Have children take one sock from a basket, find its match along the course, then pin the socks to a clothesline at the end of the course.

Observe the children continuously as they move through the course. Assist younger children if they are having difficulties. Interact with the children along the course to add excitement and appeal.

Alert the children in advance when it is their last trip through the course. Stop them one at a time as they finish the last obstacle.

School-aged children might like to help youger children move through the course.

Easier: Help younger children with obstacles beyond their abilities. Let younger children, or those with limited mobility, move between obstacles in a way that is most comfortable for them. Try constructing a course in which children must crawl and roll through the entire course.

Harder: Have school-aged children jump, hop, or tiptoe between obstacles. Allow children to skip an obstacle occasionally to enable them to pass others who are moving at a slower pace.

Variety: Change the course for variety, or to improve it, after observing how the children play. Vary the theme of the dramatic play to keep the obstacle course novel, and give the children a new purpose for moving through the course again. Plan to have the obstacle course in place for a few days to allow all children to benefit from practicing on it. Use the course as a centerpiece for day's worth of physical, academic and art activities.

Crawling through a tunnel

OBSTACLE COURSE: OUTDOOR

View On DVD

Outdoor obstacle courses can be made from outdoor play structures already available in the yard. Children love using familiar toys in new ways. Add a few low-cost items between the larger ones to vary locomotor challenges and keep the children interested.

A circular obstacle course that was quickly made from 4 laundry baskets, 3 small plastic tables, a sleeping bag, 2 hula hoops, 2 lawn chairs, a sheet, a plastic slide, mesh fabric and 7 carpet squares.

A tunnel made from three plastic patio tables draped with a sleeping bag. The tunnel exits onto a netting spider's web.

GOALS FOR CHILDREN • Practice stability • Practice running, jumping and climbing • Develop muscular strength and endurance • Learn spatial relationships • Practice sequencing tasks

EQUIPMENT

- Moveable plastic outdoor play structures such as children's slides, playhouses, and climbing structures
- Laundry baskets
- Lawn chairs, picnic benches, and any other stable, moveable lawn furniture
- Carpet squares
- Hula hoops
- Cargo netting
- Blankets, sheets or sleeping bags

Front to back: a basket to climb over; a hoop to jump into; another basket to climb over; a cave to explore and a slide to go down.

INSTRUCTIONS

Choose only pieces of equipment that you know to be safe and in good condition for children to climb on, crawl under, and go through. If you have to move a children's climbing toy, such as a playhouse or slide, be sure the toy is stable and safe to climb in its new position.

Choose obstacles that children can climb over, go under, and crawl through. Design the course so that between obstacles children have to jump from place to place and move around objects before climbing the next obstacle.

Create a course that takes the form of a loop, so the last obstacle ends at the beginning of the course. This encourages the children to go though the course repeatedly without stopping. Plan to have the obstacle course in place for a while to allow all children to benefit from practice.

Start the children through the course one child at a time. A child's plastic slide is a good place to begin. This allows children to space themselves on the course. Congestion will be limited at other obstacles along the way. Allow children to skip an obstacle occasionally so they can pass others who are moving at a slower pace.

Watch the children as they move through the course. Help younger children if they are having a hard time. Add excitement by interacting with them along the course. For example, wiggle your fingers like a spider coming toward the children when they crawl over web netting.

Let the children know in advance when it is their last loop through the course. Stop them one at a time as they finish the last obstacle.

Obstacle courses can also be created to give lots of practice jumping. Make paths of carpet squares or floor spots or bubble wrap that children jump along. Adjust the distances between carpet squares to fit the jumping abilities of the children. One way to do this is have carpet squares of two different colors. Alternate the colors on the path. Beginning jumpers jump on every square. Experienced jumpers jump only to one color, and over the other color, with each jump. This challenges the more experienced jumpers to jump twice as far as the less skilled children. Refer to **Bubble Wrap Jumping** and **On/Off** to learn jumping cues.

Jumping off a basket into a hoop

Easier: Let younger children move between obstacles in a way that is most comfortable for them. Older school-aged children can assist younger children with difficult obstacles.

Harder: Have school-aged children jump, hop, tiptoe, and gallop between obstacles. Include additional obstacles for older children.

Variety: Watch the children play on the course. Change it for variety or to improve it. Add dramatic play to make the obstacle course fun. This will give the children a purpose for moving through the course. Children love silly ideas. Pretend they are the first explorers in another land, or are seals that are lost in a jungle and have to get to the ocean. Add a sequencing task. Have the children pick a plastic egg from a basket and put it in an egg carton further along the course.

OBSTACLE COURSE: OVER, UNDER, THROUGH

Young children need to learn about spatial relationships in order to understand and follow instructions. *Over*, *under* and *through* are words that describe where things are in relation to each other. A child doing an obstacle course can go *over* the pillow, *under* the table and *through* the tunnel. The activity **Over, Under, Through** gives children a chance to learn spatial relationship terms while being physically active and having fun!

GOALS FOR CHILDREN • Practice stability
• Learn spatial relationship terms of *over, under, through*

EQUIPMENT

• Tables, chairs, pillows, sofa cushions, blankets, sleeping bags, laundry baskets, and other safe pieces of furniture and large objects to construct an indoor or outdoor obstacle course.

• Set of three homemade spatial relationship cards. Each card shows a sketch or stick figure drawing of a child either *over* an object, *under* an object, or going *through* an object such as a tunnel. Each card also has the appropriate word *OVER*, *UNDER* or *THROUGH* printed in large block letters.

On the basket

INSTRUCTIONS

Create a course that lets children safely move over, under and through various obstacles. Make a loop that lets the children complete the course close to its beginning. See the activities **Obstacle Course: Indoor** and **Obstacle Course: Outdoor** for more ideas

Spend a few minutes showing the children the spatial relationship cards. Discuss what the words over, under and through mean. See if the children can tell you whether the figure on the card is going over, under or through something.

Have the children go through the course many times. Talk about spatial relationships with the them. For example, say, "You are climbing *over* the pillows. Crawl *under* the table next." Ask the children to tell *you* how they are moving in relation to the objects on the obstacle course. Your conversations with the children about spatial relationships are the heart of this activity.

Easier: Build the course from objects that can be climbed over, crawled under, or traveled through. Use pillows, sofa cushions, laundry baskets, and furniture draped with sheets, blankets, or sleeping bags. When necessary, help younger children through the course. Encourage children with physical disabilities such as spina bifida to roll or drag themselves over and under the obstacles.

School-aged children can help younger children learn about getting through difficult obstacles.

Harder: Increase the distance between obstacles and encourage children to jump, rather than run, between obstacles. Construct the course from outdoor playhouses, slides, picnic tables and other large objects that take more effort to climb over, go under, or crawl though.

Through the tunnel and over the web

Through the hoop

79

ON/OFF

On/Off helps children develop jumping and listening skills. Play **On/Off** until children learn to follow directions correctly and can jump at least two feet. Then try **Land/Lake**. Children become much better at listening and following instructions after playing these activities. These listening skills are important skills for success in school. **On/Off** and **Land/Lake** are not elimination games. Congratulate each child for good listening.

GOALS FOR CHILDREN • Practice jumping • Learn spatial relationships • Develop listening skills

EQUIPMENT

• One carpet square or floor spot for each child

INSTRUCTIONS

Start with children standing on their own carpet squares or floor spots. Shout either "Off!" or "On!" They jump off, or remain on their spots, according to what is said. Repeat saying "On" and "Off", in any order you wish, several more times. Children must listen carefully.

Young children will need many chances before they understand that the game is really about following instructions. Children will make mistakes. Playfully redirect them to the correct position with words of encouragement.

For variety, let children who make mistakes shout the "On" and "Off" commands for a few turns while you join the activity.

This is an excellent activity for impulsive children. It requires waiting for the commands 'on' or 'off' before acting. At first it may be necessary to hold impulsive children's hands or waists to help them remember to wait until the command before acting. Do this activity often to help children develop impulse control.

Helping Children Learn to Jump

Start children jumping over low obstacles. Jumping out of a hula hoop placed flat on the floor works well. Jumping over a pool noodle is a bit harder. As the children develop their jumping skills playing **ON/OFF**, add the command "Over" so they can be challenged to jump over their carpet squares as well. When they are capable of jumping a short distance, switch and play **Land/Lake**. Refer to **Bubble Wrap Jumping** to learn more jumping cues.

Variety: Let children share turns leading the activity by saying "On!" or "Off!"

PAPER PLATE SCOOTERS

Paper plates make great pretend scooters in this easy activity. Children love pushing the plates all over. Older, taller children may find this activity harder than it is for their younger, shorter playmates!

GOALS FOR CHILDREN • Develop upper body muscular strength and endurance
• Practice stability

EQUIPMENT

- Decorative, bright colored and sturdy paper plates with attractive designs, one per child
- Objects, such as foam popsicle sticks, small stuffed animals, and picture cards to put on the paper plates while pushing

INSTRUCTIONS

Choose a carpeted area free of obstruction, large enough for children to freely scoot around safely. Let each child select a paper plate to push. Have children place both hands on their plates and begin pushing. Tell them to keep their knees off of the floor.

This activity is not meant for children who can push the plates very quickly across the floor. Friction will cause the plates to heat up and be uncomfortable for the children's hands.

Variety: Give this activity a purpose. Arrange for children to carry something on their plates from one side of the room to the other. Carrying small toys to a toy basket, or colored popsicle sticks to the proper color pieces of paper on the other side of the room work well. Combine this activity with a Carry Game. Have children scoot from one end of the room to the other and back, finding numbers or socks or Go Fish cards to match those on their paper plates.

PUSH & PULL BASKETS

View On DVD

Young children take turns sitting in a strong laundry basket as another child or an adult pushes and pulls the basket across the room or yard. Switch places and push or pull the basket back to the starting point. Children love to show off their strength!

GOALS FOR CHILDREN • Develop muscular strength • Practice working together

EQUIPMENT

- A strong, large laundry basket, big enough to hold a young child
- Heavy objects, such as books or another child, to put in the basket
- Line markers, at least 10 feet apart, at the start and end points for moving the basket

INSTRUCTIONS

Show how an empty laundry basket is easy to push and pull. Add weight, such as heavy books, to the basket or invite a child-volunteer to ride in the basket while another child, or two children working together, push and pull the basket across the room. Stay

nearby to stop the basket from tipping over. If they need it, help the children move the basket. Also help them climb in and out of the basket. Children have a tendency to push down on one side of the basket when getting out, which might cause it to tip over.

Turn on lively music and let the children push and pull the basket until all have had plenty of turns pushing, pulling and riding!

This is a great activity for including children who are unable to walk. They can practice keeping their balance while sitting in the basket, getting a 'ride.'

Variety: Pretend to 'make deliveries' of toys while pushing and pulling the laundry basket.

PUZZLE CARRY

Puzzle Carry lets young children experience different pieces going together to make a whole. Children run, or jump, or hop across the room or yard repeatedly to find puzzle pieces. Then they run back to assemble them at the starting point with your help.

GOALS FOR CHILDREN • Practice running, jumping and hopping
• Learn object, color, shape recognition

EQUIPMENT

• Puzzles with large, sturdy pieces
  Equipment Tip: Foam puzzles with just a few pieces are ideal in this activity for younger children. Wooden puzzles with about twenty pieces are best for older children.

INSTRUCTIONS

Choose several puzzles that match the abilities of the children. Scatter the puzzle pieces at the opposite side of the room or yard. School-aged children can help by placing puzzle pieces around the area. Ask the children to run across the room or yard and return with one puzzle piece per child.

When children return with puzzle pieces, ask them to guess where the piece goes. Help them place that piece in the puzzle. Send them off running or jumping across the yard or room again for another puzzle piece, until all the puzzles are completed.

Helping Children Learn to Gallop

The gallop is done while facing and moving forward with the same foot always leading and the other foot always trailing. Consider introducing the gallop after children have shown that they can do a basic run and a basic jump. Typically this will be when children are over three years of age. Show the children the gallop and encourage them to do it along side you. Place colored tape on each child's lead foot and stress that this foot always goes first. Play music with a strong, uneven beat to emphasize the uneven rhythm of the gallop.

Cues for Learning to Gallop

"Same foot stays in front." "Step-together-step-together."

Easier: Help younger children find puzzle pieces. Guide a child with visual impairments to feel and find where the puzzle pieces fit.

Harder: Ask school-aged children to gallop or skip to and from the puzzle piece pile.

Variety: Begin the activity by asking the children to take apart the pieces from completed puzzles. Have them run across the room or yard with the pieces to build a puzzle piece pile. Then do the **Puzzle Carry** activity, with children bringing the pieces back to reconstruct the puzzles.

RAINBOW PIECES

A rainbow fell from the sky and shattered into colored pieces. You were thoughtful enough to save the pieces in a bag, and now you need the children's help putting the rainbow back together again!

GOALS FOR CHILDREN • Practice stability • Learn color recognition

EQUIPMENT

- Foam popsicle sticks in many bright colors
- Colored drawing or picture of a rainbow
- 6 paper signs, one each for a color of the rainbow (red, orange, yellow, green, blue, purple)

INSTRUCTIONS

Show the children a picture of a rainbow. Ask them if they know what it is. Have they ever seen a rainbow in the sky? Can they name the colors of the rainbow? Tell them to imagine that a rainbow fell from the sky. When it hit the ground, it broke into many brightly colored pieces. You collected the pieces in a bag. Now the rainbow needs to be put back together.

Tell the children the first job is to sort the rainbow pieces into the rainbow colors. Explain what 'sorting' means. Demonstrate how you sort rainbow pieces into colors. Place the six rainbow color paper signs on one side of the floor or yard. Empty the bag of foam popsicle sticks on the opposite side of the room or yard. School-aged children can help with this task.

Ask the children to pick up one stick at a time. Then run with that foam stick back across the area and place it on the paper that is the same color as the stick. Children continue to pick up pieces until all the pieces are picked up and sorted. Then count the pieces of each color out loud with the children. If you wish, count the pieces again in another language. Ask school-aged children to gather sticks in color order: red, orange, yellow, green, blue, and purple.

Ask the children to take the sticks and place them on the floor or ground opposite the counting area, in the shape of one large rainbow. Direct them to be sure to have the colors in the correct positions, just like real rainbows. Use the rainbow drawing or picture as a guide.

Easier: Dump some rainbow pieces closer to where they will be counted, so children with less mobility, perhaps due to orthopedic impairments, won't have to move far. Assist younger children who have less skill with picking up small objects.

Harder: Challenge more skilled movers to jump, hop, gallop or skip to the pieces and back to the counting area.

Variety: Ask the children to take the sticks, one at a time, across the yard or room, and make their own rainbows.

RUNNING
WITH STREAMERS

View On DVD

When children are playing outside on a breezy day, give them crepe paper party streamers to hold as they run. They'll run like the wind! You can use this activity for spur-of-the-moment fun!

GOALS FOR CHILDREN • Practice running • Develop cardiovascular endurance

EQUIPMENT
• Several rolls of different color crepe party streamers

INSTRUCTIONS

Keep several rolls of crepe paper streamers handy for outdoor play. Tear off a six-foot section of streamer. Hold it in your hand as you move through the breeze. When the children start watching you, ask them if they would like to run with a streamer.

Explain and demonstrate the area in which it is safe for the children to run. Give the children a six-foot long section of streamer each and let them to run. Have the children bring all the streamers and any paper that broke off the streamers back to you to throw away after the activity is over.

School-aged children like this activity. Ask them to be careful not to run into younger children when playing.

Cues for Learning to Run

Just Learning: "Look where you are going." "Take big steps." "Run with your feet in a straight line."

More Experienced: "Pump your arms." "Bend your elbows." "Swing your arms forward and back, not across your body." "Lift your knees as you run."

Easier: Tell children who don't want to run that it's okay to walk with the streamers. They will see that streamers fly better when they run with them.

Harder: Show children a figure-eight pattern. Have several children run, following each other, in this pattern.

Variety: Have children run with two streamers, one in each hand. Allow a child who is blind to hold your arm while you run together holding streamers.

85

©2008 Diane Craft and Craig Smith

SOCK PLOWS

Sock Plows is an indoor activity that works well on any finished floor that isn't carpeted. Children put socks on their hands. Then they push popsicle sticks or balled paper around the floor from one side to the other.

GOALS FOR CHILDREN • Practice stability
• Develop upper body strength and endurance

EQUIPMENT

- One pair of socks per child
- Many colored foam popsicle sticks
- Many balled pieces of paper, at least 10 per child
  Equipment Tip: Ask the children to help you ball up the scrap paper.

INSTRUCTIONS

Ball up many pieces of scrap paper and store them in a bag prior to the activity. Give children each a pair of socks to put over their hands. Ask them to pretend they now have snowplows on their hands.

Tell the children that you are expecting a snowstorm in the room very soon. When the snow falls, the children must clear the room of snow by pushing it with their snowplows to one side of the room. Dump the bag of papers all over the floor as you tell the children, "It's snowing! We need snow plows to push the snow over here!" Show them the spot in the room where they are to push the 'snow.' Scoop the snow pile made by the snow plows back into the bag for some more snowy weather now or at a later time.

Easier: Make the snow from larger pieces of paper so the children will spend less time plowing. Have the children plow in a smaller area. Children who use wheelchairs with trays can push the paper 'snow' off the trays and onto the floor for other children to plow.

Harder: Make the snow from smaller pieces of paper. The activity will take longer and the children will move for more time if you drop only a few pieces of paper 'snow' for each child to plow at one time.

Variety: Substitute colored foam popsicle sticks for balled paper.

SOCK TAILS
Suggested by Marissa Patrick

A sock under a belt turns a child into a bunny! Chase the bunny and try to grab his tail!

GOALS FOR CHILDREN • Practice running • Develop cardiovascular endurance

EQUIPMENT

• One sock per child, plus
  a few extras

INSTRUCTIONS

Show children how to loosely tuck a sock under their belts, or into the top of their pants, so that the sock hangs out in the middle of their backs. Tell the children that this turns them into bunnies with tails. Ask one child to chase you to see if she can catch your tail. Let her grab the sock from your belt. Then take the sock and place it in her belt. Tell her she's the bunny now, and you have to catch her tail. Chase her and grab her tail.

When the children understand how to play, give each child a sock tail. Have the children try to grab the tails off others, without losing their own tails! Encourage children to hand back the sock tails to others so they can replace their tails and continue playing. Constantly replace tails on children as needed so they can play vigorously for a few minutes. Play lively music that goes well with chasing wild bunnies!

School-aged children can enjoy playing this tag game with each other, but not with pre-school children, who might get knocked down by the larger, faster children.

Easier: Hold the hand of a young child who is just learning to walk as he moves to catch a bunny tale. Have a 'safe' area where all bunnies are safe from tail grabbing.

Harder: Have every bunny who loses his or her tail run back to the 'tail tailor' to have a new tail put back on. You be the 'tail tailor' and keep moving around so the children have to move farther to get to you.

Variety: Ask the children to jump during the activity instead of running. Follow the activity with a snack of carrots – a bunny favorite!

SOCK THE CANS

View On
DVD

Sock the Cans is a game for practicing throwing. Children throw socks at empty cans lined up on a shelf. Like the carnival or state fair version, this one fascinates children because the cans fall over when hit, but don't fall off the shelf. Older children can reset the cans with a simple tug on a few strings!

GOALS FOR CHILDREN • Practice throwing

EQUIPMENT

- 1 can target shelf
- Many pairs of rolled children's socks
- Barrier

INSTRUCTIONS

Position the can target across two supports such as between two chair seats or picnic benches. To use the reset feature, there needs to be an open, unsupported space under the middle section of the target shelf. Make the barrier low enough to allow the children to easily throw over it. See the section on 'barriers' in Chapter 3.

Duct tape the can target shelf to the seats of the chairs or seat of the benches to hold the target in place at a comfortable throwing height for children.

Demonstrate to the children how a rolled up pair of socks will knock down cans when thrown at them. Explain that all the cans have to be knocked over before anyone goes behind the barrier to reset the cans.

Show how pulling down firmly and steadily on the strings below the shelf will reset the cans to an upright position.

Dump rolled pairs of socks in front of the barrier and let children throw them at the can targets. When all the cans are knocked down, select one child to go behind the barrier to reset the cans. No one is to throw at the target until the child resetting the cans has returned from behind the barrier! Have children take turns resetting cans.

With all of the children busily throwing, use this time to prompt children to throw with more mature patterns. Use the cue, "Bring the sock back by your ear before you throw!"

Refer to **Clean Out the Backyard: Throwing** to learn throwing cues.

Easier & Harder:
Angle the barrier so children on one end are much closer to the target than at the other end. Encourage the more mature throwers to stand farther away from the target when they throw. Have the less skilled children stand closer to the target. Children need to succeed at a task for enjoyment!

Variety: Use **Sock the Cans** as one of three or four stations that involve throwing. Line up all of the various targets for throwing and let the children throw at whatever targets they want, moving from target to target at will.

SOCK'N SMILEY

View On DVD

Sock'n Smiley is a basic throwing game that works inside or outside. Younger and older children in front of a barrier throw socks at a large Smiley Face held by an adult.

GOALS FOR CHILDREN • Practice throwing

EQUIPMENT

- 1 laundry basket
- Many pairs of rolled socks, at least 5 pairs per child.
- 1 large Smiley Face drawn on poster board
- 1 barrier

INSTRUCTIONS

Set up a throwing barrier big enough to keep children on the throwing side, away from the Smiley Face target. Make the barrier low enough to allow the children to easily throw over it. Wheeled riding toys form the barrier in this photo.

Dump the rolled socks on the throwing side of the barrier. Stand behind the barrier with the Smiley Face target and the laundry basket. Have the children throw socks at the Smiley Face. Hold the Smiley Face over the basket, so the socks drop into the basket after hitting the Smiley Face. School-aged children will enjoy holding the Smiley Face during play.

When all the pairs of socks have been thrown, invite the children to go around the barrier to pick up the socks and place them in the basket. Dump the sock-filled basket on the throwing side of the target, and have the children start throwing again.

Refer to **Clean Out the Backyard: Throwing** to learn throwing cues.

Easier: Move the Smiley Face toward the throws to make sure the socks will hit the target. Encourage children by saying things like, "Good throw," and "Oh, you hit Smiley right on the nose!" Children really enjoy throwing at a target that talks back to them! Allow children with very limited movement to drop socks from directly above the Smiley Face target, into the basket.

Harder: Angle the barrier so children on one end are much closer to the target than children at the other end. Encourage the more mature throwers and school-aged children to stand farther away from the target when they throw. Have the less-skilled children stand closer to the target. Adjust the difficulty so each child can hit the target about three out of four tries.

SPIDERS & BUGS

A big 'spider' adult chases little 'bug' children across the floor and finds the tables turned on her! Two-year-old children might not understand that they are supposed to flee from the spider. Instead, they might chase the adult who is the spider. Let them!

GOALS FOR CHILDREN • Practice stability • Develop cardiovascular endurance • Develop muscular strength and endurance

EQUIPMENT

• No equipment needed

INSTRUCTIONS

Tell the children you are going to pretend to be a big spider. The children are to pretend to be little bugs. Demonstrate how a big spider moves on all fours, with only hands and feet on the floor. Demonstrate how a little bug moves on the floor on hand and knees. Only a spider gets to move on hands and feet!

Tell the children the big spider will chase the little bugs. When the spider catches a bug, she touches the child, gently on the shoulder or back, and the child turns into a spider! Any child who has turned into a 'spider' then has to chase other 'bugs,' until all the 'bugs' have turned into 'spiders!'

Play the activity on grass or indoors. Be sure the children will not be on a surface where they might cut or skin their knees. Get on your hands and feet and start chasing little bugs! Or let them chase you! When all the 'bugs' have turned into 'spiders,' begin the game again. Be the partner of a child with a visual impariment so you can guide her as you play.

Easier: Let little children chase you, if they prefer, using any locomotor skill they choose. The younger children might not understand the concept of fleeing while being chased. No matter. As long as the children are moving around on hands and feet, or hands and knees, they will get the benefit of the physical activity. When they are a little bit older, they will grasp the concept of the game.

Harder: This game can be very tiring for children – and the adult! Use it as a quick activity sandwiched between two less strenuous activities or when you have some extra moments to fill. School-aged children might like being the spider.

Variety: Have children move like little bugs pretending to escape from a spider on one side of the yard or room to the bug's home on the other side of the area.

STILT BLOCKS
Inspired by Renée McCall

Stilt Blocks encourage children to practice balance and coordination.

GOALS FOR CHILDREN • Practice stability

EQUIPMENT

- 1 set of homemade stilt blocks per child made from:

  Two 5-inch sections of 2 x 4 board

  Lengths of rope to loop through the blocks to form a handle to hold while walking

INSTRUCTIONS

Prepare stilt blocks in advance. Cut 2 x 4 board into 5-inch lengths. Drill one 3/8-inch hole through the center of the long side of each block. Thread one piece of 3/16-inch diameter rope through the hole in the block. Tie the ends of the rope to form a continuous loop. Be sure make the rope length on some pairs of blocks longer than others because children of different heights will need different lengths of rope. Place identical marks on sets of blocks with the same length ropes. This will make it easier to identify pairs.

Give each child one block and check for proper handle lengths. Have the children walk with just one block until they are familiar with

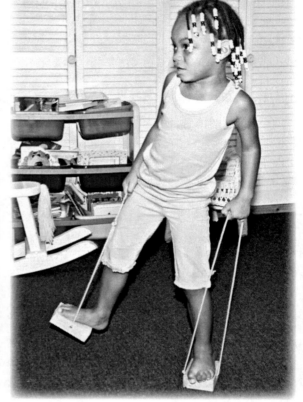

the experience of pulling up on the rope to hold the block tightly to their feet. When children seem comfortable walking on one block, give them the second stilt block to use, walking with stilt blocks under both feet. Play music that goes well with children walking!

Easier: Walk behind a child who is having trouble balancing on the blocks. Help him hold the ropes tightly as he takes steps. Cue him to walk slowly at first to feel what it's like walking on the blocks.

Don't use stilt blocks for children with physical disabilities that make walking difficult. Provide instead a flat foam pool noodle to walk on, with assistance, while the other children are walking on stilt blocks.

Harder: Set up obstacles on the floor for school-aged children to walk around.

Variety: Play a Carry Game, having children walk on stilt blocks instead of running.

STOCKING GROCERY SHELVES

When the store's shelves are empty, they have to be stocked! Children push large paper plates across the floor, delivering fruits and vegetables to stock the grocery store.

GOALS FOR CHILDREN • Practice identifying healthy foods
• Practice stability • Develop upper body strength

EQUIPMENT

- Several sets of homemade picture cards of fruits and vegetables. See how to make food cards in the activity **Healthy Food Hunting.**
- Four or five chairs, placed with their backs to the wall
- One sturdy paper plate per child

INSTRUCTIONS

Spend two minutes showing fruit and vegetable cards, one at a time. Ask children to name the fruits and vegetables as you show each card.

Explain that the local grocery store, located across the room or yard, is out of fruits and vegetables. Until more come in, each child will have to deliver fruit and vegetable cards to place on the shelves where the real fruits and vegetables will go.

Use paper plates as scooters, described in the activity **Paper Plate Scooters**. Give each child one paper plate to slide over to the store, and one fruit or vegetable card to push on the plate. Children return to get more cards until all the cards are on the shelves.

This activity is not meant for children who can push the plates very quickly across the floor. Friction will cause the plates to heat up and be uncomfortable for the children's hands.

Easier: This activity might quickly tire young children's arms. Have children who tire from pushing the plates run, jump, or tiptoe as they carry the food cards to the store.

Harder: Increase the distance children must push the plate to deliver their cards.

SWAT THE FLY

(View On DVD)

When you want preschoolers to run excitedly, try **Swat the Fly**. It takes just moments to learn the rules and boundaries. Then children charge around the play area, laughing and shouting, as they enjoy this activity! While some children drag 'flies,' made from plastic Frisbees and nylon cord, others chase them, trying to 'swat' the 'flies' with foam pool noodles.

GOALS FOR CHILDREN • Develop cardiovascular endurance • Practice striking

EQUIPMENT

- Foam pool noodles, cut in half to make two swatters
- Frisbees or vinyl plastic plates
- Nylon cord for pulling each Frisbee

  Equipment Tip: Drill a hole through a Frisbee or plate rim. Insert a four foot length of cord, and knot it under the rim. Make two copies of the 'fly,' for each Frisbee. Tape the image of the fly to each side of the Frisbee with clear packaging tape.

NOTE:

- Have drinking water on hand and watch children closely during this activity, especially during hot and humid weather!

INSTRUCTIONS

Explain to the children that some of them will drag flies, while others chase the flies, trying to swat them with foam bats. Demonstrate dragging, swatting and moving safely within the playing area. Have all children move in the same direction to avoid collisions. Explain that children may change from dragging to swatting whenever they wish.

Give some children 'flies' to drag, and the rest foam pool noodle 'swatters,' then start the activity. If anyone objects to swatting flies, put pictures of drums on the disks instead, and have children chase the drums with their foam Pool Noodle drumsticks.

Easier: Help younger children with their movement and swatting if needed. Children who are slow runners are likely to chase flies that are dragged more slowly. Children who are fast runners are likely to chase the fast flies.

Children who use wheelchairs or mobile prone standers can swat the flies that others drag past them.

Variety: For an indoor variation, make 'flies' from balloons inside netting or pantyhose. Suspend the 'flies' from an overhead structure, leaving space for swatters to swing safely. All children become swatters to practice striking.

95   ©2008 Diane Craft and Craig Smith

ZOOM, ZOOM, ZOOM

Give children each a plastic plate. Tell them it's the steering wheel of a car. Say "Go!" and watch them zoom around the yard or through the house! Combine this activity with pretending to drive around town doing errands. Children will happily drive to an imaginary store or an invisible post office for you when you ask.

GOALS FOR CHILDREN • Develop cardiovascular endurance

EQUIPMENT

- One plastic plate or Frisbee for each child to use as a steering wheel
- One STOP sign made from an old racquet or a plate attached to a stick. Write 'GO' on green construction paper, 'STOP' on red paper, and tape to each side of the racquet to make a STOP/GO sign.
- Plastic cups or cones to mark a driving lane
- One sheet of paper, an envelope, stickers for stamps and a marker for post office errands (optional)

INSTRUCTIONS

Hand the children plastic plates or Frisbees and tell them they are steering wheels. They are going to drive imaginary cars. Give them a driving lesson, showing how to start the car, back up, steer, brake and park. Show them the STOP/GO sign, and tell them green means go, red means stop. When they come up the driving lane toward you, they have to look for, and obey, the stop or go signal. School-aged children might like to take a turn directing younger children with the STOP/GO sign.

This activity gives needed practice in stopping and going on cue for children who have difficulty with impulse control.

Variety: Let the children zoom around for a while, then set out paper, stickers, and envelopes and markers at different spots in the yard or room. Ask the children to do errands for you in their cars. Have them pick up what you need to write a letter, using their best driving skills. Then have them drive to the post office to mail the letters!

Physical Activities
for Infants and Toddlers

5

Provide physical stimulation to help infants with their growth and development.

Nature has given children their own developmental schedules. At certain ages, infants begin to notice their world in more detail. As they grow, they become more able to interact with the world around them. Gradually their muscles, their brains and nerve pathways develop. Then one day they are up and walking. They have become toddlers. They can now discover much more about the world than just a few months ago when they were unable to move from the same spot on the carpet.

In this chapter we offer ways to promote physical activities among infants and toddlers from 6 to 15 months old. The information and activities here are for children who are not yet or are just becoming mobile. When children are mobile, then they are ready to join in on their own in the physical activities described in chapter 4.

Q: Are there any physical activities infants can do with the preschool children?

A: Yes. There are many ways to provide physical stimulation to help infants with their growth and development. When the other children are doing physical activities, have the infant safely off to the side so she can watch them. Whenever you can, talk to her about what is going on in the activity. When the other children are using foam puzzle pieces or plastic cards as they play a Carry Game, give the infant a safe puzzle piece or card, too. When the older children are practicing throwing at another target, hold her and let her drop balls on a target of her own.

Q: What physical activities can be done just for infants?

A: When the other children are safely playing on their own, do physical activities with the infants. These activities will stimulate motor development. Choose activities that match each infant's developmental level. Here are several activities you can do with infants.

Physical activities for 6- to 9-month-old babies: Building awareness of the world around

Encourage 6- to 9-month-old babies to be aware of their surroundings. Give them safe objects to play with, but place the objects just out of their reach. This encourages them to learn how to move themselves along the floor in whatever way they can. As babies learn to sit independently, place objects near them so they need to practice stability as they lean over and pick up the toys. Give babies safe objects to pick up, put in their mouths, handle and throw down. These activities help them develop eye-hand coordination. Also, hold babies upright so they can practice 'standing' and taking weight on their feet. Play pat-a-cake and peek-a-boo with babies who are nearly 9 months old. Try these physical activities, too.

Encourage 6- to 9-month-old babies to be aware of their surroundings.

Tug on a Sock

Hold a sock so baby grabs it. Pull lightly on the sock so baby tightens his grip. Stop pulling and let baby explore the sock. When baby drops the sock, pick it up and hold it until baby grabs it again.

Get Moving

Place the baby on her back on a blanket on the floor. Show her a favorite toy that is just out of reach. Encourage baby to wiggle, squirm, and move in any way baby can to get the toy.

Dancing with your Darling

Turn on some music and dance with baby in your arms.

Kicking Fun

Place baby on her back and hold a soft toy up to her bare feet. Encourage baby to kick the toy again and again.

Baby Kick Line

Hold baby under the arms and in an upright position. Let him kick objects and feel contact with the floor under his feet.

Sock Mystery

Place a toy, such as a rattle, three-quarters of the way inside a clean sock. Shake the rattle to make noise. Give the sock to baby and encourage her to find the rattle.

Baby Blanket Explorer

When baby can sit on his own, place him on a blanket to explore washed and clean seasonal objects. Using autumn as the example, seasonal objects could include an apple, a small pumpkin with its sharp stem removed, a squash, a shucked ear of corn, and a potato.

Pillow Obstacle Course

Place pillows and couch cushions on the floor for baby to creep, crawl, roll and climb over and around.

Provide chances for 10- to 12-month-olds to roll over on hands and knees, spy, and creep to safe, attractive objects around the room.

Physical activities for 10- to 12-month-old babies: Gaining control of the world around

At the beginning of this age range, many children can sit independently. This lets them enjoy handling and examining objects, stacking blocks, and playing with motion toys. This provides chances for 10- to 12-month-olds to roll over on hands and knees, spy, and creep to toys around the room. They are now thrilled to learn how to pull themselves to a stand, even though most are a few months away from walking without support. Encourage babies to cruise around the room, stepping while using furniture for support. As they near 12 months of age, babies may like playing with balls and other rolling objects as well as pull-toys. Climbing low heights, up to six inches, also may be a fascination at this age. Try these physical activities, too.

Where Did the Toy Go?
With baby on a blanket on the floor, put a favorite toy just out of reach. As baby watches, partially cover the toy with a cloth. Encourage baby to roll, scoot, or creep to the toy and remove the cloth to see the toy underneath.

What's in the Box?
Place a covered box, such as a shoebox with a lid, in the room with a few safe objects inside. Share the thrill when baby lifts the box's cover and finds the objects inside. Next time, place the box in another part of the room with different objects inside for baby to discover. Use the box with new objects often to stimulate baby's curiosity and motivate baby to move.

Noisy Fun!
Banging pots and lids together over and over is noisy, but doing so helps baby practice hand-eye coordination. Baby also learns about metal objects, and refines reaching and grasping skills.

What's That on Me?
Lay a flat, clean sock on baby's head, arm or leg. Ask "What's that on your head, arm, leg?" Encourage baby to grasp and remove the sock. Make it a game with you playfully placing the sock back on baby each time he removes it.

Let's Go Walking
Go walking together indoors, and outdoors during mild weather. Hold baby's hand to help her as she steps purposefully from one foot to the other in her bare feet. It may be a few more months before she begins to walk on her own. For now she is likely to really enjoy stepping with your help.

Give toddlers plenty of opportunities to walk. They will improve their walking skills as they also get healthy exercise.

Knocking Blocks Over
Build a small tower from blocks and watch baby joyfully knock it down. Rebuild it again and again so he can continue the fun while he is learning about cause and effect. You build it, he knocks it down, and you rebuild it, on and on…

Matching Practice
Let baby play with two identical plastic sipper cups. Watch her learn to put one inside the other and remove it by trial and error, as she practices her hand-eye coordination.

A Present for Me?
Fill a small box with baby's toys and let baby empty the box. Refill the box with toys and let her empty it again and again!

Baby Mountain Climbers
Lie on your back, feet flat on the floor, knees bent and drawn up toward your hips. Baby climbs up the 'mountain' made by your bent legs, and slides down onto your belly!

Physical activities for 13- to 15-month-old toddlers: Expanding the world through movement

New to being able to walk, toddlers love to hold your hand as they walk. Leave the stroller at home and instead give toddlers plenty of opportunities to walk. They will improve their walking skills as they also get healthy exercise. Toddlers are learning to share toys. Play 'give and take' as toddlers hand or roll objects to you and you hand them back. They also like the challenge of taking lids off containers to discover objects hidden inside. As children become 15 months old, they enjoy imitating adult actions, such as sweeping with a child-size broom. Many of the activities in this book build on this interest in imitation. Try these following physical activities, too.

Rolling Along
Roll a ball back and forth with toddler as you both sit on the floor.

Get that Toy
Scatter safe toys around the room. Encourage the toddler to cruise or walk around the room, moving to each of the toys to play with it.

Chase the Baby
Indoors or outdoors, enjoy playing movement games with toddler such as 'hide and seek' and 'chase the baby.'

Let's Share Toys
Hand a toy to toddler and then take it back, asking, "May I please have your toy?" Repeat again and again so she practices reaching and grasping. Hold the toy just beyond toddler's reach so she has to stretch or roll or scoot to grasp the toy.

> Provide many opportunities for infants and toddlers to move as they explore their world.

Dance Some More

Dance with a toddler while he stands, holding his arms with your hands for support. Gently dip, spin, and bob to stimulate his senses.

It's Windy!

Take toddler outdoors when a breeze is blowing. Let him feel the wind blow on his face. Talk about kites and airplanes and birds and other things that fly in the wind. Walk together with the wind and then against the wind. See which is easier.

It's Raining

In summer, take toddler outside for a brief walk in a warm, gentle rain. Cover her with an umbrella. Remove the umbrella briefly so she can feel the falling rain. Talk about the rain with her. Explain that water falling from the sky helps plants grow and gives us water to drink. While few toddlers will understand this, it doesn't hurt to give explanations about what is happening in toddler's surroundings. Be sure she does not get chilled. Help her dry off and warm up immediately after briefly getting wet in the rain.

It's Dark Outside!

If you are with a toddler at night, go outside with him when it is dark. Take a walk through the yard, holding his hand. Talk about how the sun sets and it becomes dark, but the sun will rise in the morning and it will become light again. Look up to see the stars and moon. Use a flashlight to show your toddler how light helps him see things that don't seem to be there when it is dark.

Remember:

• Provide many opportunities for infants and toddlers to move as they explore their world.

• Movement experiences will help them improve their ability to grasp, release and manipulate objects; roll over, sit up, stand, walk; twist, turn, bend, stretch and maintain their balance.

• As infants and toddlers move they will be increasing their cardiovascular endurance and muscular strength and endurance.

• All of these experiences help develop the prerequisite skills they will need to enjoy and be successful in physical activity throughout their preschool years.

The next chapter will jump ahead in age to children who are now beyond the preschool years. It discusses the physical activity needs of 6- to 12-year-olds, the 'older' kids who are already attending school.

Physical Activities
for School-Aged Children

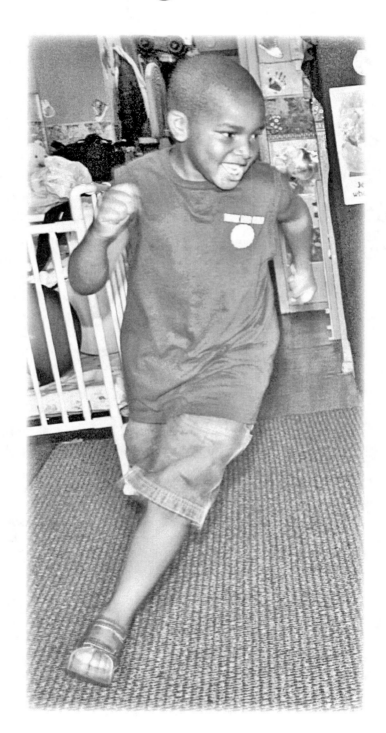

6

School-aged
children
can join the
preschoolers
in doing the
same activity,
help lead it,
or work out
on their own.

Some school-aged children 6 to 12 years of age come to childcare programs. They can be there for an hour or more before and/or after school. The same children may also come to the childcare program during the summer. Daily physical activity is very important for these children, too. They are in your care during the time when children are usually the most physically active. It is a challenge finding safe and interesting ways for school-aged children to be active around younger children. This chapter gives some ideas that may work to keep school-aged children physically active while in your care.

There are three ways for school-aged children to be physically active in childcare. School-aged children can join the preschoolers in doing the same activity, help lead it, or work out on their own. The child's age, size and attitude will usually determine which way he or she becomes involved.

When it is safe for school-aged children to join the physical activity with younger children, increase the challenge for these older children. Move them farther away from targets. Have them run longer distances. Ask them to hop, jump, gallop and slide instead of run. Let them carry heavier objects.

School-aged children who don't want to play with preschoolers might be interested in helping with the activities. Older children are good role models during physical activities. Give them special jobs. They can help set up activities. Ask them to run around putting objects in places for younger children to find. Ask them to demonstrate activities. They can run to help children having difficulties. Keep school-aged helpers active by giving them plenty to do.

Some school-aged children like doing physical activities on their own. They have favorite games and sport activities. If possible, let them do those activities on their own. Shooting baskets, jumping rope, and playing catch are some activities older children might like to do outside. Inside, they might like to learn juggling or cup stacking or dancing or just exercising by themselves.

Q: Are there physical activities in this book that school-aged children and preschoolers can play together?

A: Possibly, but it depends upon whether you feel it is safe for the older child to join in with younger children. The safety of the situation depends in part on the size, weight, coordination, and behavior of the children involved. School-aged children might be able to do the following activities alongside preschoolers. You will need to decide whether it is safe.

Alligator Pit
Bubble Wrap Jumping, if in own space
Clean Out the Backyard: Throwing

(Continued next page)

Clean Up the Floor
Frog Catcher
Hoop Limbo
Hoop Target
Hoop Scotch
Easy Kicking
Land/Lake
Obstacle Course: Indoor
Obstacle Course: Outdoor
Obstacle Course: Over, Under, Through
Easy Punching
Push & Pull Baskets
Sock the Cans
Sock'n Smiley
Stilt Blocks

Q: Can school-aged children help me lead any of this book's physical activities?

A: School-aged children might not want to do the above physical activities with the young children. Some school-aged children are so proud of being 'older' that they do not want to play games with the 'little kids.' Many others might be eager to show they are older by helping the younger children. They will happily join the physical activity as your helper. This can be a wonderful thing for everyone! The school-aged children can gain a feeling of self-worth by helping others. The preschoolers can look to the school-aged children as positive role models. And you can enjoy some help when leading the physical activities.

The following physical activities in this book have specific suggestions for school-aged children to help with the activity.

All Stop & Go to Music	Hoop Limbo
Alligator Pit	Hoop Right Through
Color Challenge	Land/Lake
Easy Catching	Laundry Pick-Up
Easy Striking	Matching Socks
Egg Farmer	Obstacle Courses
Float the Fish	On/Off
Garden Friends	Puzzle Carry
Go Fishing	Sock'n Smiley
Healthy Food Hunting	Spiders & Bugs
Hoop Chase	Zoom, Zoom, Zoom

The school-aged children can gain a feeling of self-worth by helping others. The preschoolers can look to the school-aged children as positive role models.

Six- or seven-year-olds still need lots of practice learning to do fundamental movement skills with mature form. Use the ideas listed under *Harder* in each activity to challenge older children.

Q: What if school-aged children don't want to join in activities with preschool children?

A: Fun is the main reason most children do physical activities. But what children think is fun changes as they mature! The activities in this book have all been played with 15-month to 5-year-olds. These children have had fun playing them.

Six- or seven-year-olds are close in age to preschoolers. They may still enjoy doing the same activities. Yet, most activities developed for preschoolers will be far too easy for these 6- or 7-year-olds. Six- or seven-year-olds still need lots of practice learning to do fundamental movement skills with mature form. Use the ideas listed under *Harder* in each activity to challenge older children.

Children 8 to 12 years old often like to play sports. They understand teamwork. They use their reasoning skills and can delay gratification. They also tend to focus on what their friends think of them. What was fun as a 5- and 6-year-old has become 'little kids stuff.' Give these older children a chance to do the physical activities they like. *Awesome Elementary School Physical Education Activities* (1983) by Cliff Carnes is a book that shows many physical activities for elementary school students. This book has many interesting individual and small group physical activities that use inexpensive equipment. It is available from: Cliff Carnes, Teacher In-Service, 2668 San Marin Lane, Sacramento, CA 95835, Tel. 916-483-8846.

Q: What can 8- to 12-year-olds do to be active while I am watching the younger children?

A: Here is a short list of physical activities that 8- to 12-year-olds can enjoy. They can do the activities on their own or with a few other children.

Shooting baskets: Most in 5 minutes; most in a row without missing
Keeping a soccer ball in the air without using arms or hands for 1 minute
Keeping a balloon or beach ball in the air, hitting it with hands
Jumping rope without missing for 5 minutes
Creating and/or imitating dances
Juggling scarves or rolled socks
Stacking cups
Playing active video games that use full body movements such as Wii and DDR (Dance Dance Revolution)
Standing on one leg for one minute
Doing as many sit-ups, or pull-ups, or push-ups as possible in one minute

> Ask school-aged children to pick an activity they like. Have them set goals they would like to meet for the day.

Ask school-aged children what physical activities they like. Suggest some of the activities listed above. These can be done alone or with another child their age while you are caring for the younger children. Ask school-aged children to pick an activity they like. Have them set goals they would like to meet for the day. They might choose to do the activity for a certain length of time. Or they might choose to do the activity without making a mistake. For examples, they might try to jump rope continuously or dribble a basketball without stopping for five minutes. Or perhaps see how many baskets they can make without missing.

Keep a log of school-aged children's progress. Write the name of the activity and the child's goal on a page similar to the one in figure 6.1. Call this page the child's 'Personal Best' record book. After the child has done the activity, record the results for that date. Use this record of progress to encourage the child to take on more challenges by setting more ambitious goals. It is very important to find the right challenge for school-aged children. Set the challenge too low and they become bored. Set the challenge too high and they might become frustrated due to little success. Help them find a middle ground where the challenge of the physical activity they choose is difficult, yet attainable.

Figure 6.1

Activity	Goal	Date	Results
Bounce basketball	5 minutes without stopping	Oct. 15	6 minutes!
Jump rope	3 minutes with no miss	Oct. 18	4 minutes

Remember:
• School-aged children can play activities alongside preschool children, if safe.
• School-aged children can help you with the activities by putting equipment in the right positions and by showing younger children how to play.
• School-aged children can challenge themselves by setting goals and doing harder physical activities on their own.

The next chapter has ideas for increasing children's activity levels by helping families enjoy physical activities together at home.

Physical Activities for Families

7

Tell parents about the health, developmental and social benefits physically active children experience.

This chapter gives tips on how to share what you know about physical activities with the children's families. It also gives ways to encourage families to be physically active together.

Q: What can I say to parents about providing physical activities for their children?

A: Most family adults like talking about their young children. Ask parents:

• Which physical activities do their children enjoy at home?
• Are their children already in community physical activities or sports programs?
• Would they like their children to do physical activities such as running, throwing, jumping, and kicking, with you?

Parents usually like to hear about their children's day. You may wish to mention, "We are doing daily physical activity time with the children. They are becoming fit and are learning about being healthy. They are becoming more confident about moving their bodies. And they are also learning pre-math and pre-reading skills through movement. All these things are preparing the children for school. Your child may talk about some of the physical activities we do. I have descriptions of the physical activities for you. When your child talks about the activity, you will know how to play it at home."

Q: Where do I get descriptions of the physical activities to give to the parents?

A: Family Pages describing how to do the physical activities in this book are available as a separate purchase. You may copy them and give them to parents. Two examples of these Family Pages are included here.

Q: Is there anything else I can do to get parents interested in enjoying physical activities with their children?

A: Yes. Play a familiar physical activity around the time parents begin picking up children. Parents will get to see their children enjoying physical activity. Give the parents a Family Page describing the activity you were doing at the time. Then they can do it at home with the children, if they choose.

Every few weeks, parents might also like to see copies of their school-aged children's Personal Best record page.

Remember:
• Tell parents about the health, developmental and social benefits physically active children experience.
• Give parents Family Pages so they can do the physical activities with their children at home.

ALLIGATOR PIT

Try it at home!

Crossing an alligator pit over a narrow 'bridge' is a thrilling challenge when children's arms are full and they know a hungry 'alligator' is watching their every move …

More Ideas…

Use floor spots or carpet squares as 'lily pads' laid out on the floor in a pattern. Tell the children they are 'frogs,' and must jump only on the 'lily pads' to cross the alligator pit. Chase any child who jumps into the pit.

Did You Know…

• Alligators live in the coastal swamps of North and South Carolina to the tip of southern Florida, then west along the Gulf Coast to the mouth of the Rio Grande river in Texas.

• The largest alligator ever recorded measured 19 feet 2 inches (5.8 meters) and was found in Louisiana.

• Alligators can run up to 30 miles per hour (38 kph) for a short distance.

• A healthy alligator can go many months without food.

From Alligators - Everglades National Park
www.nps.gov/archive/ever/eco/gator.htm

From Craft, D. & Smith, C. (2008) *Active Play: Fun Physical Activities for Young Children*
Available at diane.craft@cortland.edu
©2008 Diane Craft and Craig Smith

ALLIGATOR PIT

It's thrilling for young children to practice their balancing skills as they walk right in front of a hungry pretend alligator! Keep the pace of this physical activity lively to give all the children many chances to test their bravery!

how to play
•••••••••••••••••••

Ask the children to carry things you have set out, and place them in the laundry basket on the other side of the alligator pit bridge. Pretend to be the alligator and chase any children who step off the bridge, or drop something they are carrying into the alligator pit.

• *All physical activities for children require adult supervision.*

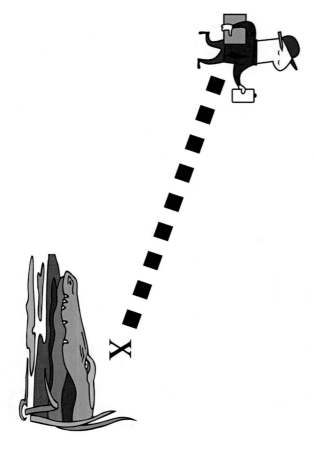

what you do
•••••••••••••••••••

Make the alligator pit by taping the 'bridge' to the floor of a room large enough for safe chasing. Place a laundry basket at the end of the 'bridge.' The adult is the 'alligator.' The alligator sits or kneels in the pit and asks each child, one at a time, to carry objects over the bridge and place them in the laundry basket. After crossing the pit, each child returns to the start for another turn by walking quickly around the edge of the pit.

• Explain that the alligator won't bother them if they stay on the bridge and don't drop anything they are carrying.

• If they drop something, or step off the bridge, the alligator will chase them with its big jaws snapping!

Make each trip more difficult by increasing the number of things each child must carry, and varying how they are carried, such as on their heads and shoulders, or between their knees.

Vary how the children must move across the pit, such as jumping, tiptoeing, or walking backward.

what you need
•••••••••••••••••••

• A 6 inch wide, 12 foot long 'bridge' **taped** to the floor. Use two pieces of flat foam pool noodles placed end-to-end, or a wooden plank, or just use masking tape to mark a 'bridge' on the floor.

• One laundry basket

• Many things to carry, such as soft toys, foam sections cut from pool noodles, or many rolled pairs of socks. Use a variety of shapes and sizes to challenge the children.

SWAT THE FLY

Try it at home!

Young children will run long and hard to catch these 'flies' and swat at them with their foam noodle flyswatters.

It's a great cardiovascular workout!

From Craft, D. & Smith, C. (2008) *Active Play: Fun Physical Activities for Young Children*
©2008 Diane Craft and Craig Smith
Available at diane.craft@cortland.edu

Did You Know...

• The best way to prevent fly problems in the home is to exclude them with screening.

• Each house fly can easily carry over one million bacteria on its body.

• Cluster flies are found during fall and winter, often in upper stories or attics. These larger flies use homes for shelter from the cold but do not reproduce inside the home. Best control includes caulking entry points and using fly swatters. If nothing is done, these flies will die on their own.

• The housefly (Musca domestica) can go through complete metamorphosis, passing from egg to larva, pupa and adult, in as few as eight days.

from *Flies in the Home*
by Barb Ogg, PhD, Extension Educator and Soni Cochran, Extension Associate, University of Nebraska Lincoln Extension in Lancaster, Nebraska

SWAT THE FLY

Give young children a healthy cardiovascular workout. Let them chase a 'fly' around outdoors in the yard or the park. Within moments children will be charging around the play area laughing and shouting and having fun!

how to play
• • • • • • • • • • • • • • • • • • •

Some children drag 'flies' along the ground while others run behind, swatting at the dragged 'fly.' Children may change from fly dragging to fly swatting whenever they wish.

• *All physical activities for children require adult supervision.*

what you do
• • • • • • • • • • • • • • • • • • •

Make enough 'flies' and 'swatters' so each child and adult can play. Make a 'fly' from an old Frisbee, or buy new Frisbees at a dollar store. Punch a small hole through the rim of the Frisbee, and tie some cord to it through the hole. Tape a drawing or photocopy of a fly to each side of the Frisbee using clear packaging tape. Use sections of foam pool noodles as 'swatters.'

• show the children the safe playing area
• show how to drag and swat
• remind children that **only** the 'fly' gets swatted
• have them choose swatting or fly dragging
• let the fun begin!

Have drinking water on hand. Be sure that the children do not become exhausted during this activity, especially during hot, humid weather.

what you need
• • • • • • • • • • • • • • • • • • •

• old or new Frisbees
• 5 foot lengths of cord
• round foam pool noodles, cut in half to make 2 swatters
• 4 inch housefly photocopies from free clip art collections on the Internet
• clear packaging tape

20 Week Physical Activity Curriculum

8

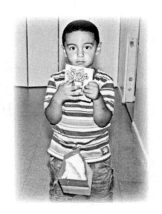

Daily
physical activity
time can help
establish a
healthy lifestyle
for the children.

This 20-week curriculum will help in planning daily structured physical activity time. The order of activities presented is only a guide. We suggest that you pick and use the activities from this book in ways that meet your needs. Start with simple activities. Add a few new activities each week. Plus, repeat ones you have done before.

Week 1

During the first week keep the physical activity time brief. Limit it to 15 minutes. From the first day, have a basic routine for physical activity time. Start by asking each child to sit on a carpet square or floor spot. Tell the children about the activity when they are sitting. Use the floor spots as the home base between each activity. Begin physical activity time with a warm-up activity. **All Stop & Go to Music** is a good choice because it teaches children to listen to musical cues. They learn to start and stop moving when the music starts and stops. End each physical activity time by singing a song together. This tells children that the structured physical activity time is done for the day.

Week 2-5

Try a different warm-up activity with the children each week. Keep the focus on helping them learn to listen and respond to instructions. Increase physical activity time by five minutes each week when you feel ready.

Week 6 and beyond

Try leading a warm-up and two physical activities from Week 6 forward. Increase the structured physical activity time until it is a full 30 minutes each day. Try new activities each week. At the end of twenty weeks you will have led 52 physical activities!

Daily physical activity time can help establish a healthy lifestyle for the children. It also gives you a chance to get regular exercise. And, both you and the children will have lots of fun along the way!

	Monday	Tuesday	Wednesday	Thursday	Friday
Week 1	Sock'n Smiley (new)	*Warm-up:* Laundry Pick-Up (new)	All Stop & Go to Music / Sock'n Smiley	**Healthy Food Hunting** (new)	**Repeat a favorite**
Week 2	Zoom, Zoom, Zoom (new)	*Warm-up:* Sock'n Smiley	On/Off or Land/Lake / Hoop Target (new)	LaundryPick-Up	**Repeat a favorite**
Week 3	**Bubble Wrap Jumping** (new)	*Warm-up:* Healthy Food Hunting	Musical Hoops / **Swat the Fly** (new) if outdoors, or **Frog Catcher** (new) if indoors	**Swat the Fly** if outdoors, or **Frog Catcher** if indoors	**Repeat a favorite**
Week 4	Push & Pull Baskets (new)	*Warm-up:* Zoom, Zoom, Zoom	Favorite Dictated Music / Sock'n Smiley	**Laundry Pick-Up**	**Repeat a favorite**
Week 5	Clean Out the Backyard: Kicking (new) if outdoors, or Clean Up the Floor (new) if indoors	*Warm-up:* **Clean Out the Backyard: Kicking** if outdoors, or **Clean Up the Floor** if indoors	Favorite Dictated Music / **Zoom, Zoom, Zoom**	Swat the Fly if outdoors, or **Frog Catcher** if indoors	**Repeat a favorite**

117

	Monday	Tuesday	Wednesday	Thursday	Friday
Week 6		*Warm-up:*	All Stop & Go to Music		
	Newspaper Toss (new) if outdoors, or **Sock'n Smiley** if indoors	**Push & Pull Baskets** **Laundry Pick-Up**	**Hoop Target** **Hoop Chase** (new) if outdoors, or **Hoop Scotch** (new) if indoors	**Healthy Food Hunting** **Swat the Fly** if outdoors, or **Frog Catcher** if indoors	**Repeat favorites**
Week 7		*Warm-up:*	On/Off or Land/Lake		
	Easy Kicking (new) **Easy Punching** (new)	**Zoom, Zoom, Zoom** **Hoop Limbo** (new)	**Easy Kicking** **Easy Punching**	**Push & Pull Baskets** **Laundry Pick-Up**	**Repeat favorites**
Week 8		*Warm-up:*	Musical Hoops		
	Clean Out the Backyard: Throwing (new) if outdoors, or **Clean Up the Floor** if indoors	**Hoop Target** **Hoop Limbo** **Hoop Chase** if outdoors, or **Hoop Scotch** if indoors	**Hoop Right Through** (new) **Swat the Fly** if outdoors, or **Frog Catcher** if indoors	**Alligator Pit** (new) **Newspaper Toss**	**Repeat favorites**
Week 9		*Warm-up:*	Favorite Dictated Music		
	Alligator Pit **Matching Numbers** (new)	**Easy Catching** (new) **Matching Numbers**	**Easy Kicking** **Easy Punching** **Easy Striking** (new)	**Hoop Bus** (new) **Hoop Limbo** **Hoop Chase** if outdoors, or **Hoop Scotch** if indoors	**Repeat favorites**
Week 10		*Warm-up:*	Favorite Dictated Music		
	Jump & Shop (new) **Sock Plows** (new)	**Newspaper Toss** **Sock Tails** (new)	**Jump & Shop** **Zoom, Zoom, Zoom**	**Easy Kicking** **Easy Punching** **Easy Striking**	**Repeat favorites**

118

Monday	Tuesday	Wednesday	Thursday	Friday
	Warm-up:			
Week 11				
Sock the Cans (new) **Sock Plows**	**Letter to a Friend** (new) **Sock the Cans**	All Stop & Go to Music **Sock Matching** (new) **Push & Pull Baskets**	**Sock Matching** **Sock Tails**	**Repeat favorites**
	Warm-up:			
Week 12				
Obstacle Course: Outdoors or Indoors (new)	**Jump & Shop Lug-a-Jug** (new) if outdoors, or **Push & Pull Baskets** if indoors	On/Off or Land/Lake **Feed the Penguin** (new) **Sock Tails**	**Obstacle Course: Outdoors or Indoors**	**Repeat favorites**
	Warm-up:			
Week 13				
Sock Tails Running with Streamers (new) if outdoors, or **Rainbow Pieces** (new) if indoors	**Alligator Pit Bubble Wrap Jumping**	Musical Hoops **Easy Catching** **Sock the Cans**	**Matching Numbers** **Newspaper Toss**	**Repeat favorites**
	Warm-up:			
Week 14				
Egg Farmer (new) **Healthy Food Hunting**	**Puzzle Carry** (new) **Swat the Fly** if outdoors, or **Bubble Wrap Jumping** if indoors	Favorite Dictated Music **Sock Matching Running with Streamers** if outdoors, or **Sock Plows** if indoors	**Spiders & Bugs** (new) **Hoop Right Through** (new)	**Repeat favorites**
	Warm-up:			
Week 15				
Float the Fish (new) if outdoors, or **Matching Numbers** if indoors	**Clean Out the Backyard: Throwing** if outdoors, or **Clean Up the Floor** if indoors	Favorite Dictated Music **Stilt Blocks** (new) **Zoom, Zoom, Zoom**	**Easy Kicking** **Easy Punching** **Easy Striking**	**Repeat favorites**

119

	Monday	Tuesday	Wednesday	Thursday	Friday
Week 16	Garden Friends (new) / Lug-a-Jug if outdoors, or Push & Pull Baskets if indoors	*Warm-up:* Clean Out the Backyard: Kicking and Throwing if outdoors, or Clean Up the Floors if indoors	All Stop & Go to Music / Stocking Grocery Shelves (new) / Bubble Wrap Jumping	Sock the Cans / Spiders & Bugs	Repeat favorites
Week 17	Easy Catching / Color Challenge (new)	*Warm-up:* Garden Friends / Alligator Pit	On/Off or Land/Lake / Go Fishing (new) / Egg Farmer	Feed the Penguin / Hoop Bus	Repeat favorites
Week 18	Obstacle Course: Under, Over, Through (new)	*Warm-up:* Stocking Grocery Shelves (using stilt blocks) / Spiders & Bugs	Musical Hoops / Letter to a Friend / Lug-a-Jug if outdooors, or Push & Pull Baskets if indooors	Paper Plate Scooters (new) / Hoop Target	Repeat favorites
Week 19	Hoop Scatter Ball (new) / Puzzle Carry	*Warm-up:* Float the Fish / Running with Streamers both if outdoors, or Clean Up theFloor if indoors	Favorite Dictated Music / Color Challenge (using paper plate scooters)	Go Fishing / Hoop Limbo / Hoop Right Through / Hoop Bus	Repeat favorites
Week 20	Letter to a Friend / Swat the Fly if outdoors, or Bubble Wrap Jumping if indoors	*Warm-up:* Obstacle Course: Under, Over, Through	Favorite Dictated Music / Rainbow Pieces / Sock Plows	Puzzle Carry / Sock Tails	Repeat favorites

References

Baughcum, A. E., Chamberlin, L. A., Deeks, C. M., Powers, S. W. & Whitaker, R. C. (2000). Maternal perceptions of overweight preschool children. *Pediatrics*, 106 (6) 1380-1386.

Brown, W. H., Pfeiffer, K. A., McIver, K. L., Dowda, M., Joao, M., Almeida, C. A., & Pate, R. R. (2006). Assessing preschool children's physical activity: The Observational System for Recording Physical Activity in Children-Preschool Version. *Research Quarterly for Exercise and Sport*, 77 (2) 167-176.

Gallahue, D. L, (1996). *Developmental physical education for today's children (3rd ed.)*. Dubuque, IA: Brown & Benchmark.

Gallahue, D. L. & Ozmun, J. C. (2002). *Understanding motor development: Infants, children, adolescents, adults (5th ed.)*. New York: McGraw-Hill.

Jensen, E. (2005). Teaching with the brain in mind (2nd ed.). Alexandria, VA: Association for Supervision and Curriculum Development.

National Association for Sport & Physical Education (NASPE). (2002). *Active start: A statement of physical activity guidelines for children birth to five years*. Reston. VA: NASPE.

National Association for Sport and Physical Education (2000). Appropriate practices in movement programs for young children ages 3-5: A position statement of the National Association for Sport and Physical Education developed by the Council on Physical Education for Young Children (COPEC). Reston, VA: Author.

Ogden, C. L., Carroll, M.D., Curtin, L. R., McDowell, M. A., Tabak, C. J., & Flegal, K. (2007). Prevelence of overweight and obesity in the United States, 1999-2004. *JAMA, 295*, 1549-1555.

Ratey, J. J. (2008). Spark: The revolutionary new science of exercise and the brain. Little, Brown.

Trost, S. G., Sirard, J.R., Dowda, M., Pfeiffer, K. A., Pate, R. R. (2003). Physical activity in overweight and nonoverweight preschool children. *International Journal of Obesity, 27*, 834-839.

Learn about fun physical activities for young children directly from Diane H. Craft. Dr. Craft is available for:

- Keynote presentations.
- Conference presentations.
- Train-the-trainer workshops.
- In-service for staff development.

Dr. Craft's presentations, workshops and trainings help groups learn to:

- Prevent/reduce obesity in young children.
- Improve fundamental movement skills and physical fitness of children.
- Use physical activity to help children learn academic concepts.
- Plan and lead 52 physical activities with toddlers and preschoolers.
- Include older and younger children as well as children with special needs.
- Encourage parents to experience the fun of physical activities with their children.

Workshops and presentations can be tailored to your needs. To discuss your requirements, please contact Diane Craft at **diane.craft@cortland.edu**

All music on *Active Play: Fun Physical Activities for Young Children* by  **on**

For more information about Vincent's music contact www.LighthouseRecords.com 1-800-897-4595

Physical Activity	Song	CD Title
All Stop & Go to Music	Song for Elizabeth	Working Together
Alligator Pit	Just One Step	Just One Step
Bubble Wrap Jumping	Double Bubble Bath	Big Bad Kitchen Band
Clean Out the Backyard: Kicking	Working Together (Pick it up)	Working Together
Clean Out the Backyard: Throwing	Working Together (Pick it up)	Working Together
Clean Up the Floor	Working Together (Pick it up)	Working Together
Easy Catching	Can I Go Outside	Big Bad Kitchen Band
Easy Kicking	I Wanna Bang on the Drum	Brand New Day
Easy Punching	I Wanna Bang on the Drum	Brand New Day
Easy Striking	I Wanna Bang on the Drum	Brand New Day
Float the Fish	River Keep Rollin' (Peaceful Village)	Working Together
Healthy Food Hunting	Questions	Read To Me
Jump & Shop	Shake, Shake	Big Bad Kitchen Band
Land/Lake	Paul's Piano	Working Together
Laundry Pick-Up	Working Together (Pick it up)	Working Together

Physical Activity	Song	CD Title
Letter to a Friend	Noon's Tune	Big Bad Kitchen Band
Lug-a-Jug	Good Morning	Good Morning
Matching Numbers	One Number Higher	Big Bad Kitchen Band
Matching Socks	Working Together (Pick it up)	Working Together
Newspaper Toss	Girls (Boys) Can Do Anything	Brand New Day
Obstacle Course: Outdoor	Girls (Boys) Can Do Anything	Brand New Day
On/Off	I Wanna Bang on the Drum	Brand New Day
Push & Pull Baskets	Music Box	Read To Me
Rainbow Pieces	Rainbow	Big Bad Kitchen Band
Running with Streamers	Can I Go Outside	Big Bad Kitchen Band
Sock the Cans	Rainbow	Big Bad Kitchen Band
Sock'n Smiley	Song for Elizabeth	Working Together
Stilt Blocks	Just One Step	Just One Step
Swat the Fly	I Wanna Bang on the Drum	Brand New Day
Zoom, Zoom, Zoom	Paul's Piano	Working Together

122

Two additional books co-authored by Dr. Craft:

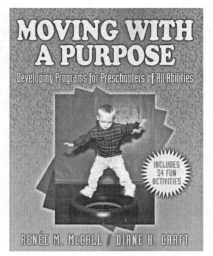

8 1/2 x 11 • 232 pages

Moving With a Purpose
Developing Programs for Preschoolers of All Abilities
by Renée M. McCall, MSEd and Diane H. Craft, PhD (Paperback - 2000)

54 ready-to-use games and activities to get preschoolers moving

15 chapters packed with information so well presented you'll be able to put it to use immediately even if you have no experience leading physical activities!

Part I explains why movement is essential for preschoolers' optimum development. **Part II** has 54 field-tested activities developed over more than 15 years teaching preschoolers. Use them anywhere, even if space, time and equipment are limited. **Part III** deepens your understanding of children's motor development and provides tips for working with toddlers. **Part IV** focuses on working with children with special needs.

Purposeful Play
Early Childhood Movement Activities on a Budget
by Renée M. McCall, MSEd and Diane H. Craft, PhD (Paperback - 2004)

A wealth of physical activities you can do with preschooler with minimal time and cost.

Create an exciting, easy-to-use physical activity program for minimal cost. This book features 36 energizing activities and 104 classroom-tested variations that use commonly available materials and require a minimum of space. Help preschoolers learn movement, fitness, and nutrition concepts while having lots of fun!

Early Childhood Movement Activities on a Budget

*Renée M. McCall
Diane H. Craft*

6 x 9 • 206 pages

Please make check payable to: **Active Play Books**
and mail completed order form with payment to:

Diane Craft • 10 Wheeler Avenue • Cortland, NY 13045
Tel.: 607-591-1757 • email: diane.craft@cortland.edu

✂ •

# of Copies	Title — ORDER FORM	$ Each (USD)	Subtotal	
	Moving with a Purpose: Developing Programs for Preschoolers of All Abilities	29.00		①
	Purposeful Play: Early Childhood Movement Activities on a Budget	24.00		②

Add postage and handling charge (1st book $4.00; $2.00 for each additional book): ③

NY State residents add 8% NYS Sales Tax on book and S&H total - or include tax exempt form: ④

TOTAL DUE (1 + 2 + 3 + 4):

SHIP TO:

(Please print) **NAME** _____

MAILING ADDRESS _____

CITY _____ **STATE** _____ **ZIP** _____

Thank You!

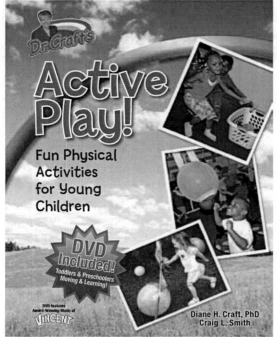

81/2 x 11 • 132 pages

DVD showing 30 of the book's
52 physical activities is included
with the book

Active Play!
Fun Physical Activities for Young Children
by Diane H. Craft, PhD and Craig L. Smith (Paperback - 2008)

Audiences: *Childcare Providers in centers and homes, Preschool Teachers, Special Educators, and Therapists*

Active, healthy lifetimes start with physically active children!

The 52 physical activities in Active Play! are
- created for toddlers and preschoolers to play together!
- easy to lead, fun to do!
- inexpensive, using easy-to-get equipment!
- designed for children to develop fundamental movement skills and physical fitness!
- inclusive of children with special needs!

8 1/2 x 11 • 132 pages with DVD showing 30 physical activities

This book and DVD set:
- Shows how to make physical activities irresistable.
- Teaches academic concepts through physical activity.
- Includes a chapter of physical activities for infants, 6 months to 15 months of age.
- Includes physical activities for school-aged children.

See how easy it is to lead fun, inexpensive and effective physical activities that benefit every young child!

# of Copies	Title	ORDER FORM	$ Each (USD)	Subtotal	
	Active Play! Fun Physical Activities for Young Children - BOOK and DVD		39.00		①
	Add postage and handling charge (1st book $ 4.00; $ 2.00 for each additional book):				②
	NY State residents add 8% NYS Sales Tax on book and S&H total - or include tax exempt form:				③
		TOTAL DUE (1 + 2 + 3):			

Please make check payable to: **Active Play Books**
and mail completed order form with payment to:

Diane Craft • 10 Wheeler Avenue • Cortland, NY 13045

Tel.: 607-591-1757 • email: drcraft@activeplaybooks.com

SHIP TO:

(Please print) **NAME** _____

MAILING ADDRESS _____

CITY _____ **STATE** _____ **ZIP** _____

Thank You!